DANCE!

A Complete Guide
to Social, Folk, & Square
Dancing

This is a volume in the Books for Libraries collection

DANCE

See last pages of this volume for a complete list of titles.

DANCE!

A Complete Guide
to Social, Folk, & Square
Dancing

J. Tillman Hall

AYER COMPANY, PUBLISHERS, INC.
SALEM, NEW HAMPSHIRE 03079

Reprint Edition, 1988
Ayer Company, Publishers, Inc.
382 Main Street
Salem, New Hampshire 03079

Editorial Supervision: Janet Byrne

———

Reprint Edition 1980 by Books for Libraries, A Division of Arno Press Inc.

Copyright © 1963 by Wadsworth Publishing Company, Inc.

Reprinted by permission of J. Tillman Hall

Reprinted from a copy in the University of Illinois Library

DANCE
ISBN for complete set: 0-8369-9275-X
See last pages of this volume for titles.

Manufactured in the United States of America

———

Library of Congress Cataloging in Publication Data

Hall, J   Tillman.
   Dance! : A complete guide to social, folk & square
dancing.

   (Dance)
   Reprint of the ed. published by Wadsworth Pub. Co.,
Belmont, Calif.
   Bibliography: p.
   Includes indexes.
   1. Folk dancing--Study and teaching. 2. Square
dancing--Study and teaching. 3. Dancing--Study and
teaching. 4. Ballroom dancing--Study and teaching.
I. Title. II. Series.
[GV1743.H28 1980] 793.3'07   79-7766
ISBN 0-8369-9294-6

DANCE!

A Complete Guide
to Social, Folk, & Square
Dancing

DANCE!

a Complete Guide
to Social, Folk, & Square
Dancing

by J. Tillman Hall, University of Southern California

Wadsworth Publishing Company · Belmont, California

All music scores are reprinted by permission from *Physical Education in the Elementary Schools* by Winifred Van Hagen, Genevie Dexter, and Jesse Feiring Williams (California State Department of Education, 1951).

DANCE! A COMPLETE GUIDE TO
SOCIAL, FOLK, AND SQUARE DANCING
by J. Tillman Hall

Printed in the United States of America

To

Louise, Nancy, Jody,

and

the Westchester Lariats

Foreword

This book is a product of Dr. Hall's long and extensive experience in working with children and adults. He has taught thousands of youngsters to dance for the sheer joy of dancing. And they have learned not only the techniques of dance but also its history. They have learned about people throughout the world—why they dance and what they dance.

For more than ten years the author has directed a performing group of recreational dancers, the "Westchester Lariats." About five hundred young people have been members of this group for a year or more. These dancers have performed all over the United States and have often appeared on television.

It has been my privilege to witness in these dancers the development of aesthetic values, self-confidence, pleasure in cooperative fun and work, social efficiency, and physical skill. The author has been highly successful in capturing the interest, cooperation, and imagination not only of the dancers and their parents but of a great segment of the population of a large community.

The dances that appear in this book are selections from a large repertoire of dances which the author has found to be the most popular for true recreational dance purposes. These are the dances that dancers enjoy performing and that audiences enjoy watching.

Aileene Lockhart
University of Southern California

Contents

Preface

Man has always used dance to express his emotions and beliefs about the world, society, and his life in general. This book follows the development of dance from man's primitive beginning to his civilized position in today's world. The historical approach seems necessary if a complete understanding of recreational dance is to be achieved.

Many people involved in teaching dance have little or no professional training in the field. I have often watched beginners struggling to interpret dance materials that were written primarily for experienced professionals. The materials in this book have been organized and written with the untrained person in mind.

Beginning teachers of dance often have difficulty deciding which dances the participants will enjoy. This book contains dances I have found to be the most popular over many years of observation. Most of these dances have been taught in all parts of the United States, and their descriptions are those most representative of the fundamental movements of the dances. A few dances have been simplified for recreational purposes. Readers wishing to compare these descriptions with other versions should consult the references listed with the dances and the sources listed in the bibliography.

Thanks and appreciation are expressed to all those who have contributed towards my understanding of recreational dance. To those whom I have had the pleasure of teaching I extend my most humble appreciation. From each of them I have learned many things.

Special recognition and appreciation are extended to Mr. John Youman for his development of the chapters on softshoe and tap dancing. His assistance in the development of other phases of this manuscript has been most helpful. Sincere appreciation is extended to Mrs. Louise Hall for her help in transcribing the music, Dr. Aileene Lockhart for her Foreword, Mrs. Laura Setter for her typing of the manuscript, Mrs. Timmie Perstein for her art work in the descriptions of the social dance steps, Mr. Cecil Lynch for his photography, Mr. John Klein for his assistance with the chapter on music, and Bob Sorani, Jan Arborgast, Denny Nolan, Jill Speed, Nancy and Jody Hall, Nancy Conover, and all of the Lariats for their help in developing many of the dances.

Appreciation is also extended to those who gave permission to use special materials in this manuscript.

Thanks are due Mrs. Esther Hurn for her costume development as used in the photographs; to Dr. and Mrs. Noel Shutt, Mrs. Cecil Lynch, Mrs. Alma Conover, Mrs. Barbara Escallier, Mrs. Virginia Stevens, Mr. Bill McNee, Mr. and Mrs. Gene Colvin, Mr. and Mrs. Henry Mills, Dr. and Mrs. Abe Maurer, Mr. and Mrs. Laverne Erickson, Mrs. Regina Greenleaf, Mrs. Jane Kuska, Mrs. Margaret Arpin, Mr. and Mrs. Don Harrison, Mrs. Madeline Palotay, Mr. and Mrs. Clyde Giroux, Mrs. Arnie Gunderson, Miss Ellie Walsh, Mrs. Bessie McNee, Mrs. Alice Downs, Mrs. Mary Ann Arcella, Mrs. Jan Klein, Mrs. Helen Fromme, Mrs. Lynn Gary, and the executive committee of the Westchester Lariats for their devoted help with this project.

Finally, special recognition is given to Dr. Elwood Davis for his continued prodding to keep me working on the manuscript, and to Dr. Aileene Lockhart, Dr. Lois Ellefeldt, Dr. Lenore Smith, Dr. Lola Sadlo, Miss Pat Remnick, Miss Ruth Anderson, Mr. Meredith Willson, Mr. Lawrence Welk, Mr. Art Linkletter, Mr. Al Jarvis, Mrs. Francis Chapman, and many others who in some way contributed to this manuscript.

J. Tillman Hall

DANCE!

A Complete Guide
to Social, Folk, & Square
Dancing

1

the

History

of

Dance

The exact length of time that man has inhabited the earth will probably never be determined. But whether man has lived on earth a few thousands or many millions of years, his concern for various forms of rhythmical activity has influenced his existence from the beginning.

PRIMITIVE MAN

It is presumed that primitive man's wisdom was limited to the knowledge gained through the use of the five senses. The action he observed in the world around him was frequently beyond his ability to comprehend. Nevertheless, he must have observed the rhythm exhibited by the movement of the sun and the moon, the stars and planets. Furthermore, the length of days, nights, winters, and summers, the fall of the rain, the beat of the heart, and the chatter of birds must have left indelible impressions in his mind concerning the rhythmical evolution of the universe and its inhabitants.

Regardless of the authority with which historians seem to write, what we know about the folkways of primitive man is largely guesswork. However, it is educated guesswork, arrived at from numerous logical clues.

Primitive communication. It is assumed that during prehistoric times, before vocal language was invented, sign language and gestures were the chief means of communication. As primitive men banded together to protect themselves from a hostile world, they developed the art of gesturing as the predominant tool of communication. With vocal language consisting of a few grunts and groans, gestures would have had to resemble actual events with considerable accuracy if true meaning was to be communicated.

When primitive man tried to communicate through gestures to his fellow men he must have done so in a rhythmical manner. If he gestured the chase and kill of an animal, for example, he doubtless imitated the actions of both himself and the animal. Thus, language had its beginning with these communicative gestures.

Thousands of years must have passed before prehistoric man developed talents in speaking and writing. During this period, the art of imitation was developed to a much greater degree than one commonly finds exhibited in today's society. Moreover, it is presumed that primitive man used his entire body in gesturing. This presumption is based on the theory that, in general, refined movements of separate parts of the human body were not developed until a much later date in history. This concept could in many ways be challenged. Still, it is well recognized that perceptual-motor learning is usually quite complex and involves a retention of the effects of past experiences in such a way as to modify later behavior.

The reader may better understand primitive man's communicative problems by trying to relate by gesture such experiences as the fear of a fire, dizziness, a headache, the struggle with a crocodile, or any experience that might have confronted primitive man.

Primitive dance. When gestures and body movements began to fall into a regular or irregular pattern, caused by the occurrence of accented beats and movements, man had created dance. Basically, the flow of movement or procedure with uniform recurrence of cadence, beat, accent, and composition denotes rhythm. *Dancing is expressing one's beliefs and emotions through movement disciplined by rhythm.*

Many antiquarians and historians believe that the most enjoyable and important activity in the life of primitive man was his dance. We know that he had special dances for almost every important occasion, such as birth, acceptance of young people into adulthood, marriage, and death. He had dances for courage before battle and dances to celebrate victory. It was through dance that primitive man seemed to meet the challenge of his environment and to obtain new power.

Will Durant suggests that primitive man sang before he learned to talk and that he danced as early as he sang (Durant,* *Our Oriental Heritage,* p. 88). He further points out that no art so characterized or expressed primitive man's emotion as did the dance. It gradually developed from primordial simplicity to a complexity seldom rivaled in civilization.

WHAT IS DANCE?

A series of movements and steps, rhythmically performed and timed to music. is called dance. It consists of bodily actions conveying sundry ideas in both dramatic and rhythmic form. It is often described as being the first art because it is the earliest impulse that takes on an outward embodiment. Among primitive man it always had some accompaniment by means of which the rhythm was emphasized. This accompaniment consisted of clapping the hands, chanting, beating a drum, hitting two rocks or sticks together, and so on. The instruments used in making music and in keeping time were limited in range and accomplishment but were endless in variety. Native ingenuity exhausted itself in fashioning such instruments as horns, skins, trumpets, gongs, clappers, tom-toms, rattles, castanets, and flutes. The taut string of the bow was probably the origin of the lyre and the violin. Even today's opera and drama can be traced to the music, song, and dance of primitive man.

An eminent authority on dance states:

> The dance inherited from savage ancestors as an ordered expression in motion of the exhilaration of the soul, develops and broadens into the search for God, into the conscious effort to become a part of those powers beyond the might of man which control our destinies. The dance becomes a sacrificial rite, a charm, a prayer and a prophetic vision. It summons and dispels the forces of nature, heals the sick, links the dead to the charm of their descendants; it assures sustenance, luck in chase, victory in battle; it blesses the fields and the tribe. It is creator, preserver, steward and guardian.†

Urlin states that the origin of all dances seems to be based on at least three principles (Urlin, p. xii).

> 1. Ceremonial or religious dancing, imitative of the movements of the spheres, as they were called in ancient cosmogony.
> 2. Dramatic or histrionic representations of man's chief passions—love and war—with other primitive themes as a basis.
> 3. Mimicry, or imitation of the movements of animals as an outcome of the belief in animal ancestry.

* Full information on source references can be found in the Bibliography at the end of this book.

† Curt Sachs, *World History of the Dance* (New York: W. W. Norton & Co., Inc., 1937), p. 4. Reprinted by permission.

FROM THE ANCIENT WORLD TO THE RENAISSANCE

Ancient man danced primarily for ceremonial purposes, even though he was expressing his emotions at the same time. Allusions to dance are found in the records of almost every age and nation, whether barbarous or civilized. Earlier historians believed that barbarians had the strongest passions and were most easily affected by rhythmical sounds (Ferrero, p. 21). Sounds that to us might be unmusical, such as the drumming of sticks on a hollow log or blowing on reeds incapable of yielding a musical note, were very addictive and agreeable to these primitive men.

Biblical times. The Scriptures contain ample evidence that there were a considerable number of celebrated events at which the ancient Hebrews danced. David, king of the Jews, danced in the presence of all his people. The Israelites danced at the inauguration of the golden calf. Christ, in narrating the parable of the prodigal son, refers to music and dancing. The Hebrews gave dance a high and important place in their ceremony of worship. Moses, after crossing the Red Sea, bade the children of Israel dance. Solomon said there is "a time to weep, and a time to laugh; a time to mourn, and a time to dance." Dancing is also frequently alluded to in the books of both Matthew and Luke.

Early Egyptian dance. Egyptian engravings of 6,000 years ago reveal the use of dance in religious rituals. The Egyptians believed that their gods danced; thus, magic and religion inspired most of their early dances. One of the most interesting and best known of ancient Egyptian dances was the astronomical dance, performed by a priest. This particular dance emphasized the harmony of the universe. The stars, moon, planets, sun, and earth were all represented by rhythmic movement throughout the exhibition.

Most of the foot and hand movements currently used in dance are identical to those used by the Egyptians in their dances several thousand years ago. It is said that the pirouettes, jelles, coupes, and caprioles of today originated with the Egyptians.

The dance in Ancient Greece. The Greeks through their ingenuity and elegant taste polished and refined the art of dancing so that it stimulated considerable emotional excitement in the minds of spectators. The Greeks combined dance and choral singing into one art. Plato described dancing as the desire to explain words through body gestures. It has been said that the Greek warriors at Troy danced as they fought, thus making it more difficult to be hit by a lance. Socrates danced and maintained that it was one of the very best ways to develop and retain physical health (Durant, *The Life of Greece*, p. 229).

The Greeks developed several different forms of drama and dance. Among the stage dances were Emmeleia, the tragedy; Kordax, the comedy; Sikinnis, the satirical drama; and Pyrrhic, the weapon dance (*World Book*, Vol. 4, p. 18).

The ballet was introduced at an early period in Athens. After the ballet had been introduced, a ballet master was considered an indispensable requisite. This person was required to be not only a practical musician but a judge of composition, if not a composer himself. Later on the requirements were raised to such an extent that the ballet master had to possess universal knowledge. He had to master poetry, music, geometry, philosophy, rhetoric, painting, and sculpture.

Training in dance seems to have been far more vigorously pursued in Sparta than in any other place in Greece. The Spartan philosophy was basically a training to produce a warlike people. Thus their dances were vigorous, gymnastic, and purposeful for their particular society. Their war dances developed into exhibitions to display the skill and art of their performers.

The funeral dance, performed by the Greeks and later the Romans, indicates how ideas were passed from the ancient Egyptians to later societies. In this dance a mimic, dressed in the dead person's clothes and wearing a mask that resembled the dead person's face, preceded the funeral procession. The mimic portrayed the dead person performing his best-known deeds.

The philosophers and writers of Greece strongly recommended that all pupils be taught dance for its beneficial effects on both body and mind. It was considered a means of giving soldiers carriage, agility, health, and cultivation of esprit de corps. Attention was called to the beauty of harmonized movements of healthy bodies.

The Greeks invented the use of scenery, music, and costumes, which achieved effects undreamed of in earlier times. They also believed that the gods gave a great deal of attention to the dance. Therefore, most of their productions were staffed by professional dancers who enjoyed great prestige.

Plutarch said that the military dance was an indefinable stimulus that inflamed courage and gave strength to persevere in the paths of honor and valor (Kinney, p. 14). It seems that perfectly timed drills used by the Greek soldiers had a demoralizing effect on their enemies in battle. These drills most certainly had great disciplinary effect on the Greek soldier. The movements of the military dance were highly acrobatic and were identical to those used in battle.

The Greeks brought together poetry, music, dancing, grouping, posing, and—perhaps most important of all—the pantomime. They used numerous props such as castanets, cymbals, tambourines, and masks to identify various characters.

Simple rustic dances were not omitted; they were used to celebrate the gathering of crops and the blossoming of flowers. Also, dances suggesting the life of various animals were very popular.

Perhaps the best-known dances of ancient Greece are the Kolia (a broken circle dance), Dance of the Spilled Meal, Spear Dance, Shadow Dance (in which the dancer fights a mock battle with his shadow), Hymeneia (danced to celebrate a well-conducted wedding), Kordax (mimic drunkenness), and Sikinnis (a dance drama).

From the tenth century to the second century B.C., Greece was truly the center of the world's most cultured civilizations. However, because of her struggles with Persia and the conflicts arising among the city states, she fell prey to and became a part of the great Roman Empire in 146 B.C.

Greek dances popular in the United States are Gerakina, Hasapikos, and Kalamatianos—the Greek national dance.

Roman influence. The Romans did not add very much new material to the dance. After becoming rulers of the Mediterranean world they fostered the presentation of dances from other nations. However, they did develop the pantomime, which they found in Greece and Asia Minor, to a high degree of efficiency. The Romans did very little dancing themselves—they were spectators rather than participants—but they brought in dancers from all the nations that they conquered. In fact, Roman leaders made many disparaging remarks about dance; they thought it unfit for persons of importance.

The Dark Ages. With the declination of the Roman Empire, dancing, like all the arts, almost passed out of existence. There was a gradual retardation in social, political, and intellectual development, which was characterized by a great cultural retrogression. Christian monasticism was practically the only source of academic learning. All physical activities, which included dance, were censured by the monks as being worldly and paganistic. Thus, with the Dark Ages, aesthetic interest declined and gave way to asceticism. Monastic life was regarded by many as being the only worthwhile way to live. Nevertheless, the institution that conserved choreography through the brutishness of the Dark Ages was the Church.

The Renaissance and the Reformation. The Renaissance began to bring about a refreshing influence in all areas of dance. Feudalism gave way to monarchy, and warfare gave way to peaceful coexistence. Exclusive interest in religion began to diminish, and greater emphasis was placed on human beings; thus humanism was born. The humanist writers—Petrarch, Boccaccio, Colet, and More—because of the success of knighthood recommended all kinds of vigorous exercise. This attitude opened the door for a rebirth of interest in all phases of dance.

Consequently, with the beginning of the Reformation, freedom to pursue leisure-time activities for the sake of pure enjoyment was not only tolerated but actually encouraged. Of course all people did not immediately accept these principles; even today there are groups who disapprove of this philosophy. But it has gradually gained in popularity and approval over the centuries.

Durant summarizes the interest in dance during the Reformation as follows:

> Of all the pastimes the best beloved was the dance. "After dinner," says Rabelais, "they all went tag-rag together to the willowy grove, where, on the green grass, to the sound of merry flutes and pleasant bagpipes, they danced so gallantly that it was a sweet and heavenly sport to see." So in England, on May Day, villagers gathered round a gaily decorated Maypole, danced their lusty rustic measures, and then, it appears, indulged in intimacies reminiscent of the Roman festival of Flora, goddess of flowers. Under Henry VIII the May games usually included the Morris (i.e., Moorish) dance, which had come from the Spanish Moors via the Spanish fandango with castanets. Students danced so boisterously at Oxford and Cambridge that William Wykeham had to forbid the ecstasy near chapel statuary. Luther approved of dancing, and relished especially the "square dance, with friendly bows, embracings, and hearty swinging of the part-

ners." The grave Melanchthon danced; and at Leipzig, in the sixteenth century, the city fathers regularly held a ball to permit students to become acquainted with the most honorable and elegant daughters of magnates, senators, and citizens. Charles VI often led the ballet or dance at the French court; Catherine de Medici brought Italian dancers to France, and there, in the later days of that unhappy queen mother, dancing developed new aristocratic forms. Dancing, said Jean Tabourot, in one of the oldest books on one of the oldest arts, "is practiced in order to see whether lovers are healthy and suitable for one another; at the end of the dance the gentleman is permitted to kiss his mistress in order that he may be as certain if she has agreeable breath." In this manner . . . dancing becomes necessary for the good government of society. It was through its accompaniment of the dance that music developed from its vocal and choral forms into the instrumental composition that made it the dominating art of our time.*

Since the Reformation, there has been a continuous trend towards a greater variety of dances along with a greater number of participants each year. Almost every country in the world has made unique contributions to the field of dance; some have even received universal attention.

ASIA SINCE THE RENAISSANCE

Most Asian dancing in the United States is performed by ethnic groups. Some schools and folk-dance clubs learn a few dances from countries such as India, China, and Japan. However, most of the dances with the greatest popular appeal in the United States have originated either in Europe or in the Western Hemisphere. Our discussion of Oriental dance is therefore limited to a general background of the Asian contribution to world dance.

Japan. Most traditional Japanese dances are based on mythology and are ceremonial in origin. The sun dance and the flower dance are typical of the worship of nature that existed in ancient Japan. The dance of present-day Japan may be divided into two broad classes: (1) the modern or popular and (2) the special or professional. The popular is the one most commonly used for recreation. The special or professional is very exciting and requires many years to master. It is usually dramatic, and much effort is made to reveal the inner feelings of joy, anger, sorrow, and love, through the music or through rhythmic movements. Perhaps the best-known professional dances are the Cherry Blossom Dance, performed by charming geisha girls, and the kabuki dances. Kabuki dancers have an international reputation for their ability as actors as well.

Japanese dancers usually use some prop such as a fan, scarf, ribbons, or umbrella to add special effects to their dances. The professional dancers wear exotic costumes and are known for the most extensive application of facial cosmetics seen anywhere.

Recently, considerable interest has developed in such Western ballroom dances as the waltz, the two-step, and swing. This was probably an outcome of the American occupation of Japan following World War II.

* Will Durant, *The Reformation* (New York: Simon and Schuster, 1957), p. 70. Copyright © 1957 by Will Durant. Reprinted by permission.

India. India's dances are best known for their dramatic form—a sort of pantomime in which a story is told by means of gestures. Indian dancing is highly stylized and has its own vocabulary, which defines the movements of the hands, eyes, and body. It requires rigid muscle control, perhaps more than any other dancing in the world. There are more than twenty finger movements for each hand, each movement having a different meaning. In most of the dances the lower limbs have less important movements. Frequently the dances are accompanied by song, and body gestures dramatize the words of the song.

Dancers in India are to a certain extent trained by performers of their own caste and sex. Training is started early in life and requires many years of hard work if the student is to become a good dancer. Music, dancing, and acting, like other professions in India, are usually passed on from parents to children.

Nautch dancing, a very difficult exhibition dance performed by professionals, is based on religious mysticism. It portrays the legend of the God Krishna and his wife Rahda—their meeting and their love for one another.

Other important dances of India are hunting dances, war dances, and rainy-season dances (dealing with growing and harvesting). There are also many native dances dealing with the portrayal of demons and devils. Whether their purpose was originally to flatter the devils and demons or to drive them away is not known. There are also many dances meant to drive away specific diseases.

China. Several thousand years ago the inhabitants of China displayed considerable interest in dance. Records indicate that there were traveling dance companies specializing in dances believed to hold healing power for various diseases (Shawn, *Gods Who Dance*, p. 47). However in more recent times, dance has lost its appeal to the Chinese and today is found to be rather uninspiring. Social dance does not seem to be very popular in any of the Asian countries, and this is especially so in China. The few dances seen in China mime civil life and war. They are mostly acrobatic in style.

Burma. The dances of Burma are charming and appealing. They seem to use a mixture of all dance movements along with a considerable amount of acrobatic styling. Many of these Burmese dances contain steps performed from a squatting position similar to some of the Russian dances.

THE MIDDLE EAST SINCE THE RENAISSANCE

Israel. Dances of Israel have been more popular in the United States than those of any other Far or Middle East country. Practically all of the Israeli dances performed here are similar in nature and are basically chain and circle dances. Some of the most popular Israeli dances are Ken Yovdu, Hineh Ma Tov, Dundai, Adarin, Yemina Yemina, Simi Dundai, Kumu Echa, and the Harmonica.

Turkey. Perhaps the most popular dance from Turkey is Chupurliki. As in other countries of the Middle East, the chain dance seems to be the most popular formation for most of the dances.

Other dances from the Middle East which have gained wide interest are those performed by the Dancing Dervishes, a religious group composed of Mohammedan monks. Their dances are considered a form of folk dance. Another group, the Whirling Dervishes, spin like a top, often becoming so hypnotized by their own movement that they go to sleep while performing.

EUROPE SINCE THE RENAISSANCE

Most of the countries of Europe have contributed either complete dances, individual steps, or specific styling, all of which have greatly influenced dance in the United States. As the Renaissance spread westward from country to country, so did the interest in dance.

LATIN INFLUENCE

The Latin-speaking nations of Europe are Italy, Spain, Portugal, France, Rumania,* and a portion of Switzerland. The term "Latin-speaking nations" generally refers to the peoples or countries whose languages and cultures are derived from the ancient Roman civilization.

Italy. Ever since the Renaissance, Italian interest in dance has been constantly on an incline. Currently, dancing may be seen almost everywhere and on almost every occasion. The Italians have assimilated dances from those of all other nations.

The great similarity among most Italian dances is probably due to the overwhelming influence of the Catholic Church. Originally, many of the dances of Italy were performed to singing, chanting, and humming. However, today the musicians that accompany the dancers play on ancient types of pipes, mandolins, guitars, and the most popular instrument, the accordian. The Italians are fond of singing and are particularly partial to tunes in 6/8 time.

The Italians have many chain and circle dances that are similar to those found in other parts of Europe. A very popular dance, the Duru Duru, has an onomatopoeic title that denotes the sound of the palm of the hand beating a tambourine. The introduction of the music to this dance is in 2/4 time, while the remainder of the dance is in 6/8 time.

Northern dances such as the Trescone, the Bergamasca, the Pavane, the Monferrina, the Trivili, and the Furlana change into the gayer and freer Saltarello of central Italy, which again gives way to the love-making, fiery Tarantella of the south. The Saltarello is perhaps the most famous couple dance of Italy.

The Tarantella is perhaps the best-known dance to have originated in Italy. Each region tends to have its own version of this dance. The original version is found in Sardinia. The traditional meaning indicates that it was a curative dance in which a person who had been bitten by the tarantula attempted to expel the poison by going into rapid twirling movements, using strenuous exercise as an antidote. However, the movements of this

* Because Rumanian dances are more closely related to those of Slavic nations than to those of Latin, Rumania will be discussed with the Slavs.

dance have been greatly exaggerated through theatrical demonstrations. Later versions link this dance to courting dances in which there is a great deal of flattery and a final love conquest. Italian dances are frequently in 6/8 time and consist of high hops, long hops, and many heel-and-toe steps, accompanied by the ever-popular tambourine.

Other popular dances of Italy include the Taratata and the Spadonari di San Giorio; both are exciting sword dances.

Spain. Since earliest times the dances of Spain have been very popular. They have been divided into two schools: the Iberian, known as the classical, and the Gypsy, known as the flamenco. Spain has probably had as many conquerors as any other nation, and each one has brought characteristics that to some extent have flavored the dance of that country. Perhaps the Moorish influence, which dominated Spain for about seven hundred years, has had the strongest influence on both dance and music.

Spanish dances are famous for solo acts by both men and women. The women as they dance exhibit various emotions as they flip their shawls, fans, or skirts in a spirited manner. The men's solos display considerable complicated footwork and acrobatic movements.

The flamenco, which the gypsies made famous in Spain, is composed of broken rhythms and cadences accompanied by the dancer's foot taps and hand claps.

The saraband originated in the solo dances of twelfth-century Spain. Its footwork is little more than slow glides. The dance remained popular because it conformed to the court etiquette of the Renaissance.

Some Spanish dances have not changed in more than a thousand years. The earliest known dances were the Turdion (a comical dance with prescribed foot movements), the Gibidana, the Piedegibao, the Madama Orleans, the Alemana, and the Pavana. Later on, the Saraband, the Chacona, the Bolero, the Fandango, the Seguidilla, and the Jota became popular. Lately, the most popular dances seem to be the Jaleo de Jerez, the Palotea, the Pola, the Gallegada, the Muyneria, the Habas Verdes, the Zapateado, the Zorongo, the Vita, the Tirano, and the Tripola Trapola. Many of these dances are composed of steps found in the original Fandango and the Seguidilla. Some of the most popular Spanish folk dances done in the United States are Fado Blanquita, La Madre Del Cordero, Jota Tipica, and Jota Aragonesa.

Portugal. There is no single dance or costume to represent Portugal. Her dances are similar to those of Spain, the Fandango and the Fado being among the oldest and most popular.

France. It has been said that France is the nursery of dance, the Eden of the grand ballet. Very few dances are French in origin. Instead, dances from other countries that were brought to France were perfected under the systematic French leadership in this field. France is of a greater mixed ancestry than is the United States; therefore, her dance is varied. Throughout history she has been in a perpetual state of war both internally and externally. Nevertheless, as a result of intermarriage and of historical events, her interracial people have been welded into ethnic groups so that many of her dances, once highly distinctive, today closely resemble each other.

French dances are simple, the steps are easy, and the dancers are neat, self-restrained and very careful of their behavior. These characteristics are probably due to the fact that down through the ages the French have had the opportunity to present their skills in dancing before their own royalty.

There were very few dances worthy of mention before the Renaissance in France. During the sixteenth century the two major types were the basse danse and the haute danse. In the basse danse the dancer's feet did not leave the floor. The steps were highly stylized and elegant. There were five basic foot positions for the many basse danses. In the haute danse, all known dance steps were included along with numerous hops, leaps, high jumps, kicks, and stamps. The basse danse and the branle double appear to have been very similar to our fox trot and two-step. The branle simple also resembled our fox trot except that it contained three kick steps immediately following the single step.

Later on in the seventeenth and eighteenth centuries the gaillarde and the volta were introduced from Italy and the pavane was imported from Spain. The pavane and the branle were extremely popular and were frequently referred to as the kissing dances. Perhaps this added to their popularity.

A very popular court dance was the courante, which was performed on tiptoes and contained many bows and curtsies. It has been said that both the minuet and the waltz, to some degree, were derived from this dance, and it, in turn, was similar to the seguidilla of Spain. Noblemen of France, to be in fashion, had to master the courante.

The ancient contre-dances of France were brought to England and changed to country dances; the French versions appear to have been the root of our modern-day quadrilles. The contre-dances were generally performed by four couples and consisted of a variety of movements.

Perhaps the dance that the French brought to the greatest stage of perfection was the minuet. Its origin was rustic, yet it was polished and molded into a perfect expression of the deportment of the court society. The minuet as presented by touring exhibition groups is not the same as the original minuet of France. The steps, as currently presented, are more varied and difficult.

Other popular dances of France were the Gavotte and the Cotillion. They were both rustic in origin and required considerable polishing before they became popular court dances. Originally the gavotte consisted of a collection of very difficult folk-dance steps, but as time passed the dance was simplified so that anyone could learn the movements. La Bourrée, a French clog-dance, contained considerable hand clapping, finger snapping, energetic movements, and shouts of enjoyment. The farandole, a chain dance, has been very popular in southern France. French dances that have become popular in the United States are La Robe Du Chat, Sur Le Bord De La Rivière, Garçon Volage, and Polka Piquée.

The ballet had its origin in Italy but reached an artistic peak under the direction of the French teachers.

THE SLAVS

Russia, Yugoslavia, Poland, Czechoslovakia, and Bulgaria, along with other fringe nationalities composed of Sorbs, Slovaks, Serbians, Croats, and

Slovenes, make up the Slavic-speaking peoples of Europe. Their ancestors were descendants of the nomadic tribes that spread all over Europe immediately following the receding of the last ice-cap that covered this area. Until about 800 A.D., these tribes were moving their flocks from one place to another, constantly searching for adequate summer and winter pastures. About this time they began to settle in permanent localities and attempted to defend themselves from migrating warlike expeditions. Despite considerable differences in tribal characteristics, they developed and retained one specific form of dance, the kolo (Lawson, p. 73).

Although Rumania is not one of the Slavic-speaking nations, Rumanian dances resemble those of her Slovakian neighbors more than they do those of the other Latin-speaking countries. Dance is one of the major Sunday afternoon activities. On various occasions, chains of dancers may be seen performing a serpentine hora throughout the village streets. Other popular dances are the sarba and the calusari. The hora indicates early Greek influence, while the calusari dates back to the ritual dances of the neolithic period.

Russia. The dances of Russia are varied and peculiar to this Slavic nation. They consist of impetuous acrobatic action and are characteristic in many ways of the rustic life of the people. Most of the dances are of a chain form in which the steps become more complex as the dance progresses. In America, the best-known Russian dances are the Pletyonka (a chain dance), the Korobushka, the Russian Peasant Dance, the Hopak, and the popular Troika. Other Russian dances that are included in many school curriculums are the Kolomyka, the Kamarinskaia, the Scherr, and the courtly Alexandrovsky.

Other Slavic dances. The two most common forms of dance in the Slavic nations are the kolo and the hora. Both are circle or chain dances in which the leader often dictates the type of figure to be danced.

In Yugoslavia, the uninhibited movement of cat-like steps of the kolo has inspired many variations of this popular dance. As the dance begins, the tenseness and alertness of the dancers are evident. Then as the dance progresses, the dancers become more relaxed and fade into collective rhythm from which they seem never to tire.

Perhaps the most important Yugoslavian dances are the Padushka (a Macedonian chain dance), the Troyanats (a circle dance made up of numerous tiny steps and jumps), the Zhikino Kolo, the Devojacko Kolo (very popular in the Serbian mountain region), and the Neda Grivny. Yugoslavian dances popular in the United States are the Seljancica Kolo, the Milica Kolo, the Kozacko Kolo, and the Kukunjeste Kolo.

Other popular dances of the Slavic nations are the Karakoviak, the Polonaise, the Goralski Taniec, the Mazurka, and the Kujaviak of Poland. All of these dances have the accent on the second beat of the music.

Czechoslovakia relies mostly on the Kolo and the Hora as forms of dance. But perhaps her most popular dance is the Janoshka, a recruiting dance in which occupational skills of the armed services are demonstrated.

Some other Slavic dances that are popular in the United States are the Polka, the Schottische, the Cobbler Dance, the Bohemian Rovenacka, and the Moravian Kaca and Reznik. The most popular Bulgarian dance is the Rachenitsa. This dance is one in which the strength and endurance of the

men are tested through a display of agility in movement. The women are expected to keep up with their partners by executing tiny hops or small running steps.

Several internationally popular folk dances originated in the three small countries of Lithuania, Latvia, and Estonia, which are now part of the USSR. Some of the most popular dances that came from this part of the world are Sustas, Ziogelis, Kubilas, Sukcius, Wooden Shoes, Sadala Polka, Eide Ratas, Kalvelis, and Sudmalinas.

FINNO-UGRIANS

"Finno-Ugrian" refers to the people and language of Finland and Hungary. Their language is a subfamily of the Ural-Altaic languages, which include Finnish, Magyar, and Estonian.

Finland. The Finnish folk dances of today were the ballroom dances of yesterday. The most important folk dances are those performed at weddings. Other dances that are quite popular are Purpuri (which consists of many figures, each having its own tune), Taneli, Sahan Katrilli, and Sjalaskuttan (the seal's jump). The dances are composed of mazurka, polka, and schottische steps, intermingled with gliding, walking, running, galloping, and hopping.

Hungary. Hungarian dances are similar to those of Poland, performed in open or closed circles or longways sets. Many of the dances contain unique features, such as quick, snapping foot movements, clipping of the heels together, jumping and clicking of the heels together in the air, and so on.

Hungary's most popular contribution has been the Czardas. It consists of quick draw steps, turns, and bokazos (the special name for heel-clicks).

Other areas in which Hungarians have made noteworthy contributions are recruiting dances, wedding dances, and theatrical dances. The Hungarians are well known for their unique contributions in a number of interesting craftsmen's dances. Some of these portray the skill involved in cooking, in weaving, and in the use of weapons.

ALPINE COUNTRIES

High in the Alps, which run through Switzerland and Austria, are many different stocks of people who have, however, many folklore similarities. Their dances are energetic and peculiar to this section of the world.

Some of the most popular dances in the Alpine countries are the Rheinländer, the Schuhplattler, the Mazurka, and the Weggis.

TEUTONS

"Teuton" designates the Northern European language groups of Scandinavian countries, Germany, the Netherlands, Belgium, and portions of the English and French population.

Germany. Dance has been forbidden periodically more often in Germany than in any other European country. The dance that was censured more than any other was the turning-couple dance, similar to our present-day social dances.

Perhaps Germany's most important contribution to the field of dance was the German cotillion, later called the German. The cotillion is not a single dance but rather a display of round and social dance instruction, along with meticulously planned instructions in etiquette. The cotillion was organized to the extent that the number of ladies equaled the number of gentlemen in each group. Basic fundamentals were taught in the waltz, the galop, and the polka. The leader or conductor of the cotillion determined the number of dancers and the order of dances for each program. He carefully supervised all the participants to ensure maximum development in skills, manners, and general deportment. There was a great variety of dances for each cotillion; in fact, one source listed 250 different dances (Lawson, p. 157).

During the seventeenth century the waltz became very popular with the bourgeois society in Austria and Germany. The French claim that the volta was the mother of the waltz. However, most authorities give credit to Germany for origin of the waltz. In its infancy, the waltz was accepted with great reluctance in many countries. It was considered immoral, suggestive, and indecent to hold a girl in a social-dance position and twirl around over the dance floor. But finally, in the nineteenth century, the waltz became one of the most popular and most accepted kinds of dance, and its prestige has not waned since that time.

Other German dances that have become very popular in the United States are the Viennese Waltz, the Galop, the Rheinländer, the Cobbler's Dance, Kinderpolka, Klapptanz, Spinnradl, Siebenschritt, Hansel and Gretel, Come Let Us Be Joyful, the Bohemian Polka, and the Schuhplattler.

Sweden and Norway. Sweden and Norway were one kingdom until the twentieth century, when they became separate nations with different kings and ruling bodies. However, their customs, dance, and folkways in general have always been very similar.

Sweden has been the leader in the revival of many old Scandinavian dances that were practically smothered out by the polka. Some of the most popular folk dances in the United States are among those that have been revived. Many of the dances are unique in step and sequence. They have simple melodies peculiar to those specific countries.

Some of the most popular Scandinavian dances are Daldans (a dance pantomimic of taming women), the Nixie Polka (a fairy dance), Carrousel, Bleking, Vingakersdans (a dance in which two women are competing for the same man), Klappdans, Gustav's skoal (a quadrille), Tantoli, Norwegian Mountain March, Oxdansen (a mock battle), Snoa, Snurrbocken, Hambo, Hambopolska, Landskrona Kadrilj, and Frydasdal Polska. All of these dances have become very popular in the United States and are found in many school curriculums.

Denmark. Perhaps Denmark's most unusual folk dances are the Mallebrok, the Crested Hen, the Hatter, the "Little Man in a Fix," Seven Jumps, and the Tinker's Dance. All of these dances are popular in the United States.

England. Owing to the research of Cecil Sharpe, much of England's folklore and many of her folk dances have been recovered. It was chiefly through his efforts at the beginning of the twentieth century that considerable interest in the revival of folk dance was developed.

Perhaps the oldest and simplest forms of English folk dance were those performed in a closed circle. As the rituals at which these dances were performed became more involved, the movements of the dances became more complicated. From the closed circle the chain dance evolved. It was originally believed that the gap in the circle was essential so that evil could escape and good could enter. Thus magic was an important element in the ritual dances.

After the development of chain dances, the processional march and the promenade became popular. It is believed that they were originally used to ensure continued favor and fertility from the governing spirits. The entire community participated in the English processionals. They formed a long line, weaving in and out of houses, sweeping with tree branches everything in sight. Sometimes the dancers moved in single file, but usually they were in double lines.

English milkmaids' dance on May Day.

Research has revealed that there were two main types of ritual dances in England: the Sword Dance and the Morris Dance. Originally, they were both danced by men. The Sword Dance was very popular in the northeastern part of England. It was performed in a ring formation consisting of from five to eight dancers. Each person carried his own sword in his right hand and held the point of another person's sword in front of him with his left hand. As the dancers moved around in a circle they performed intricate movements by dancing around, over, and under their swords, never releasing their grips on their own and their neighbors' swords. Eventually the swords were interlaced in such a way that they formed a shield. The locked swords were then placed around the head of a make-believe victim. After the group danced around the victim for awhile, each person would draw his own sword from the magic shield in a way that symbolized the decapitation of the victim.

Urlin remarks that the sword dance was accompanied by wild music on the bagpipes and by shrill cries from the performers (Urlin, p. 100).

The Morris Dance was one of the most popular in the midland counties of England. It is commonly believed to have originated in ancient fertility rites. The dance was usually performed by six men, and frequently accompanied by a fool or a clown. The costume was very simple and differed from town to town. It was usually made of bright colors, with ribbons hanging from the dancers' hats and bells strapped to each leg. Dancers usually held a stick or white handkerchief in each hand. They always colored their faces so they could not be recognized. These dances supposedly contained magic, and were often used for remedial purposes. Typical instruments used to accompany the Morris Dance were the pipe and tabor (a drum), both played by one person. The pipe was held with the left hand and the drum was beat with the right. The English differ from most peoples of the world in that they do not have any traditional costumes. Their dances are performed in the dress of the period.

When Henry VIII broke all ties with the Pope and declared himself head of the English Church, dancing became very popular throughout England. Henry was an enthusiastic supporter of dance.

English dance steps consist of little more than skipping, sliding, and smooth running or walking steps.

England, like many countries, has several processional dances that are very popular on certain days of the year. One of their most popular is the Maypole dance.

Other popular English dances performed in the United States are Gathering Peascods, Rufty-Tufty, Sellenger's Round, Green Sleeves, Black Nag, Sweet Kate, Morris Jig, Shepherd's Hey, Circassian Circle, Dargason, and Rhif Wyth.

Scotland. Down through the years Scotland has maintained a unique clan system which has influenced the dress, education, folkways, and dance of each succeeding generation. In 1746, Prince Charles Stewart tried to put an end to the clan system, the playing of bagpipes, and the wearing of the Highland costume. However, as usual, edicts such as this tended to pull the Scottish clans together and make them more determined than ever to wear their costumes and to dance.

Scotland has many festivals where the kilted laddies and lassies dance the internationally popular Highland Fling, which symbolizes victory or rejoicing, and the Sword Dance, which was originally performed on the eve of battle as a means of relieving tension. Another popular Scottish dance is the Reel of Tullock; legend places the origin of this reel in a country church where one cold wintry day the people danced to keep warm while they waited for the minister to arrive. Other popular native dances are the Highland Schottische, the Strathspey, and numerous three-, four-, and eight-hand reels.

Ireland. The Irish have two distinct styles of dance. In one, the dance can be described as recreational, because there is much romping, laughter, and community spirit displayed. In the second, the dancers display fine technical skill and unique body movements. The upper part of the body is held erect while practically all skill movements are executed with the feet.

Irish dances are most frequently composed of taps, stomps, shuffles, hops, and step-hops. Some of the most popular are the Irish Lilt, the Waves of Tory, Cor Na Sidheogh (the Fairy Reel), Rinnce Mor (the Seven), the Irish Reel, the Kerry Dance, and numerous jigs, reels, and hornpipes.

Jigs and hornpipes have a great deal in common and are composed chiefly of clogging and shuffling movements. They are performed with the body held erect and arms at sides, while the feet produce a variety of tones by taps of heels and soles on the floor and against each other.

The Netherlands. The Dutch are an agricultural people; thus their folklore is rustic and their dances are simple. Some of the most popular Dutch dances are Zomervreugd (summer joy), Baanopstekker (bean stalking), Peer Desprong (horse jumping), and Myn Wagen (my wagon).

MEXICO AND SOUTH AMERICA

All the countries south of the United States have retained their native music, dress, and dance, which partially reflect the characteristics of their ancient heritage.

Mexico. Dancing has flourished in Mexico since the days of Aztec supremacy, when houses of song and dance were located near the temples. The Aztec dance teachers lived in these houses. Dance was required of everyone over twelve years of age. Those who did not attend dance classes regularly were severely punished. The arts of dance and music were essential to the success of Aztec festivals.

Numerous Indian dances such as Los Viejitos (the little old men) are still very popular in Mexico. This dance has strong religious implications despite its comical appearance. Its basic intention was to discourage people from becoming old and inactive.

Other popular Mexican dances are Las Virginias, La Mosca, La Costilla, Jarabe Ranchero, Jarabe Tapatio, Chiapanecas, Mi Pecosita, and La Raspa.

South America. Indian tribes such as the Incas of Peru and the Amazons of Brazil developed many dances, most of which were extremely primitive. Many would be judged obscene by civilized societies. A considerable number of the dances were symbolic of ancient paganistic beliefs, and they should be viewed in this light.

After the Spanish conquest, the conquistadores greatly influenced dance in South America. During the eighteenth and nineteenth centuries, fiestas and celebrations became important in the culture. Accounts of those events clearly identify their relationship with their Spanish heritage. The natives used many kinds of guitars along with a host of percussion instruments in accompanying their dances and festivals.

The twentieth century brought forth a great surge of interest in polyrhythms and syncopation. In spite of social problems—which have brought discontent and, in some countries, revolution—the Latins have remained keenly interested in music and dance. Some of their creations have become popular throughout the world. Their best-known dances are the Rhumba, the Tango, the Cha Cha Cha, the Samba, the Merengue, and the Calypso.

From the thirteenth to the fifteenth century, most of the people in Europe were seeking personal answers about the legends of the Saints. Their minds were steeped in mysticism while, on the other hand, their personal desires were inflamed with materialistic ambitions. This strange combination of beliefs and desires happened to be the proper mixture to initiate the most expansive era in history. Additional factors such as the breakdown of the feudal system, epidemics of bubonic plague, the desire for religious freedom, continuous wars, inflation, and the general loss of integrity and hope helped to set the stage for the discovery of the New World. All the virtues that had been responsible for the establishment of order out of the chaotic Dark Ages had suddenly lost their charm in a period when almost any sin could be remitted for a price. Thus we see the conditions and the exposed minds of many of the people who discovered and migrated to the New World.

If we are to understand the place of dance and folklore in America, its meaning and importance, we must understand the conditions under which the people existed and what they did as they tried to re-establish the dignity of man. We must understand that as the colonies of the New World grew they encompassed the traditions and customs of more and more nationalities. And they were also influenced by the culture of the American Indian. Dance in America gradually grew to reflect these diverse cultures and is thus a synthesis of dance throughout the world.

Authorities have pointed out that, except for the Puritans, the early colonists were not against dancing. In fact, they respected and admired dance. But they disapproved of mixed dancing. They were fearful that men and women dancing together might create uncontrollable social problems.

The Puritans objected to dancing on religious grounds, owing to their Calvinistic interpretation of the Bible. The Maypole, for example, was considered a heathen idol, and those who performed around it were considered to be practicing paganistic worship. The Puritans also felt that professional performances were sinful and professional performers immoral. For this reason it was not until the middle of the eighteenth century that professional entertainment troupes from Europe arrived in the United States. Also, early dancing masters were not the most reputable people in the New World, and their questionable activities cast a shadow on the early development of dance.

However, the Puritans could not keep the inevitable from happening. Educators in England had begun to write about the importance of dance. Sir Thomas Elyot in *The Book Named the Governour,* Roger Ascham in *The Scholemaster,* John Milton in his *Tractate on Education,* John Locke in *Some Thoughts Concerning Education,* Charles Morton in *Compendium Physicae,* and John Playford's *The English Dancing Master* all emphasized the values of dance. These books made their way to America and stimulated interest in the dance. People gradually began to realize that dance developed many desirable attributes, such as good manners and behavior, attractive carriage, and graceful movements.

Patriotic pageants were stressed in the period immediately following the American Revolution. These pageants often included some kind of dancing, as well as demonstrations of acrobatics.

One of the most unusual dance exhibitions during this time was used in the ceremonies of the Shakers. The Shakers were a religious sect that had at first settled in the New England states and later migrated as far south as Kentucky. They originally came from England. Their religious faith barred them from marriage and from all sexual relationships. Their major purpose was to create a sinless society in the New World.

Usually they formed small communities and conducted their business in a socialistic manner. Some would farm, while others would be assigned various occupations within the settlement. They made practically every tool and piece of equipment they used. In fact, they were recognized for their outstanding craftsmanship in all fields of work. Some of their inventions were far more advanced than those in general use by other people of their times.

A Shaker service.

Their dance followed basic square-dance form with the exception that the men and women performed in separate groups. They believed that by shaking as they did in their dances they could shake sin out of their bodies.

The Shakers contributed nothing new to the field of dance, but they did keep alive the idea of dance as a basic part of religion—an idea that has perhaps made our society a little more tolerant than it otherwise might have been.

Permission to reproduce the picture of the Shakers in one of their services was granted by Mrs. Curry Hall, president of the Shaker Museum in Auburn, Kentucky. Those traveling in this vicinity would be rewarded by a visit to this museum.

Although the immigrants of New England came to the New World for religious freedom, those of the Southern colonies came for economic reasons. These colonies therefore had less restriction in establishing interest in dance. During the eighteenth century dance became one of the most popular activities in Southern schools. Well-known physical educators such as Dio Lewis, Catherine Beecher, François Delsarte, William G. Anderson, and Dr. Dudley A. Sargent did much for its promotion as an acceptable activity in the physical education curriculum.

COSTUMES

The various types and parts of folk-dance costumes originated with various nationalities. A brief discussion of some of the basic parts of native costumes seems significant in a study of the history of recreational dance.

Costumes developed as a result of two main factors: (1) the belief in evil supernatural beings and (2) geographical and climatic conditions.

Clothing gave man protection against unknown forces. He used color and ornamental designs sewn into the cloth, as well as beads, bracelets, and other pieces of jewelry, to ward off evil spirits. He also used costume accessories as symbols; for example, the cock's feathers stuck in a performer's hat were symbols in the old mating dance.

The types of cloth used for costumes were determined not only by climatic conditions but also by the country's crops or products. In Egypt the main garments were made of cotton, which was the principal crop raised in that country. In Europe, where flax grows well, the garments were made of linen. Wool was widely used in colder climates, and silks were most popular in areas where silkworms were cultivated.

As mankind divided into classes, based on upper and lower statuses, costumes were used to display the wearer's status and wealth. Color and ornamentation were more elaborate in the higher strata of society.

By the time the Renaissance was in full bloom, all the basic garments, such as the apron, overjacket, smock, and trousers, were known and used throughout Europe.

The apron or overskirt, originally used to protect the body, was later decorated and used to protect the dress. It also gave the girl an opportunity to display her ability in needlework.

As people became more industrious they learned to make overcoats and jackets from furs, skins, and leaves, thus adding protection and comfort. Because they believed in magic, they created decorative and often quite artistic symbols and designs.

The basic smock or shirt of the Slavic countries was originally worn for protection against rain, cold, and insect bites.

The headdress had its origin in court fashions.

Trousers were the last basic part of costumes to be developed. They were added by the nomadic herdsmen as a more suitable garment for horsemen.

The type of dance performed and the costume worn at any stage of history relates closely to the customs, beliefs, and environment of the people. By studying the history of dance one can gain insight into the history of man. How he dressed, worked, played, thought, and worshipped are exemplified by how he danced.

We have seen that dance originated with primitive man's attempt to communicate and that it developed in the rituals of ancient civilizations. As these civilizations developed, the ancient folk dances were refined and polished until they were used for recreational purposes. Then the dances became segregated into different forms and styles of presentation. At each step of man's progress, someone always attempted to fight new ideas and prevent new forms and types of dance. However, such types as ballet, social dance, square dance, modern dance, tap dance, jazz dance, and an endless variety of others have continually developed and perhaps always will.

The twentieth century has seen a crystallization of all forms of dance. Its values and future will be discussed in succeeding chapters. Its past has been briefly described. Those wishing further knowledge should consult the sources listed at the end of this book.

2
the
Values
of
Dance

Since the beginning of civilization, thinking people have expressed beliefs that an individual could derive inestimable values from learning how to dance. In our age of satellites, astronauts, spaceships, missiles, and the harnessing of atomic energy, society has drifted dangerously toward the theory that values that cannot be scientifically measured are values of secondary importance. From this scientific viewpoint it is very difficult to measure the importance of activities such as dance. However, some measurements are possible. An educated guess by a professional trained in the fine arts can determine to a reliable degree what values may exist in a specific experience.

25

For centuries, educators such as Thomas Elyot, Roger Ascham, John Milton, John Bunyan, and John Locke have emphasized the values inherent in learning how to dance. In our century the Educational Policies Commission in *Education for All American Youth* and Holger Kilander in *Health for Modern Living* have reminded us of these values.

Most of the values can be grouped under three headings—*sociological, physiological,* and *psychological.* Several of the inextricable attributes could of course be treated under two or more categories. In this case, the attribute has been placed under the one that seems to present the most inescapable value.

Recreational dance includes a wide range of choice and movement. Notwithstanding the exceptional, references on values relate to those types of dance—such as folk, square, social, and round—that are most commonly used in recreational situations. However, other forms—such as tap, ballet, modern, and creative dance—are just as recreational, and offer many of the same values.

SOCIOLOGICAL VALUES

It is generally recognized that in every experience there are numerous simultaneous learnings. An individual may derive one, none, or a cluster of values from any given experience. The values derived, seemingly, are dependent upon the nature of the individual and his reservoir of capabilities at any given time. These capabilities depend, of course, on his inheritance, experience, environment, stimulation, satisfaction, and opportunity to utilize the learnings. Consequently, the values that radiate from learning to dance are subject to all these incalculable variables.

Personality development. Everyone recognizes the importance of a winning personality. Personality is usually evaluated on the basis of how a person accepts and reacts to society and, at the same time, how society accepts and reacts to him. An individual recognized as having an integrated personality is one who has satisfactorily adjusted himself to his social environment. He is alert, he thinks quickly and can shift the focus of his attention without losing perspective, he has workable ideas based on sound judgment, and he is not afraid to take a stand on basic issues.

The integration of a person's physical, spiritual, social, emotional, aesthetic, moral, and cultural life into a harmonious function has always been a challenge to educators. All persons and agencies concerned with the enlightenment of an individual are vitally concerned with the development of the personality. Parents and teachers are constantly guiding young people into experiences that will aid in this development. Recommended experiences for this achievement have naturally been quite varied. However, many of the world's leaders and educators have indicated that learning to dance very definitely contributes toward the development of an integrated personality.

Society tends to approve individuals who possess graceful and purposeful movements—the type of movements that demonstrate poise. Almost any kind of dance, properly taught, contributes to the development of poise, refines manners, and improves bodily carriage. The development of these traits is essential to the achievement of an adjusted, integrated personality.

Activities that offer opportunities for the participant to learn leadership and "followership" are enriching experiences. These activities should be conducted so that they teach the participant tolerance and respect for the abilities of others. Seldom does an individual master these traits easily. Learning to dance can bring the individual into contact with a number of distressing emotional situations—situations that teachers must be aware of and able to control. Learning to dance is rewarding if the social environment under which the learning takes place is controlled.

It is essential that physical and social skills be taught concurrently, so that manners, attitudes, and courtesies become basic to dance experiences. Dance is an activity in which one can learn social responsibilities and creditable behavior traits as well as make new friends and be drawn closely into a social group.

PHYSIOLOGICAL VALUES

The physical body is composed of millions of tiny cells that depend on activity for their development. Before modern technology made us slaves of the push-button, adequate physical activity was possible through the movements encountered in everyday life. However, it has been substantiated through the Kraus-Webber tests, military examinations, increase in mental health problems, increase in cardio-vascular disturbances, obesity, and numerous other indices, that the vitality and stamina of the human race are on the decline. The future health of civilization depends on a physically strong human body. The medical profession and physiologists in general strongly recommend a substantial increase of activity for the majority of people.

Some of the specific physiological contributions of exercise in dance are discussed below.

Physical fitness. The term "physical fitness" is relative, but, in general, it implies a feeling of well-being. It is characterized by energy, stamina, and agility. Of course, all people need not have the physical fitness of a champion athlete; but they should have more than they need merely to maintain their livelihood. Far too many people are so tired when their normal day's work is completed that they cannot really enjoy their earned leisure time. The maintenance of physical fitness should be a continuous process. It is not something that, once achieved, requires no further effort.

Adequate exercise generally assures improved functioning of all the body organs, thereby eliminating many causes of fatigue. The circulation of the blood, the exchange of oxygen in the lungs, and the peristaltic movements of the intestines are but a few of the processes affected and improved by maintenance of physical fitness.

The organic system is in turn dependent on adequate functioning of the muscular and nervous systems. And they in turn depend on adequate activity, sufficient rest, and proper nourishment as a basis for their work. Adequate exercise promotes both a healthy appetite and sound sleep. An advantage of dance as a form of exercise is that it is adaptable to any age and ability.

Suppleness. One of the greatest physiological contributions of dance is in the maintenance of body suppleness. As the body grows older, there is a continuous tightening of the muscles and ligaments, gradually restricting movements and causing tension. In dance these ligaments and muscles are stretched and suppleness is maintained.

Coordination. Coordination is essential in developing any physical skill. To achieve coordination, the muscles of the body must work harmoniously together. Most people know very little about the kinesiological action of the muscles. In most instances, they learn by trial and error. A good teacher and demonstrator can be invaluable in defining specific movements through activities such as dance.

Posture. Maintaining good posture is a distinct problem because the human skeleton is fundamentally unstable in the upright position. To maintain this upright position, the skeleton must continually battle the effects of fatigue, the pull of gravity, and the false comfort of hanging on its ligaments.

Poor posture, however, contributes to the inefficiency of body organs. It also creates personality problems, because posture is often looked upon as the keystone to good health and attractiveness.

Dance, unlike many other recreational activities, emphasizes good posture and promotes its maintenance through the skills involved in the activity.

PSYCHOLOGICAL VALUES

For many years psychologists and sociologists have been writing about relaxation, confidence, self-evaluation, wholesome attitudes, and recognition as being essential to mental health. Just to talk about these attributes does very little good. Everybody needs the opportunity to experience them in real life.

Relaxation. Tension is a term denoting upsets in the steady state of the body—upsets often caused by stress. Anxiety, irritability, incoordination, and hyperactivity are symptoms of built-up tension. Unresolved tensions may have a harmful effect upon health.

Most people build up a certain amount of nervous tension every day. Unless this tension has an opportunity to escape, basic nervous problems arise. Mental breakdowns may be caused by built-up tension. Dance offers an excellent opportunity for the release of pent-up emotions.

Young people need an opportunity to participate in wholesome recreational activities in which over-eager parents and teachers cannot dictate every move that a child makes. It is important that there be time for activities in which everyone has an opportunity to lose himself in play. In such activities most emotions are dispelled.

The technical emphasis in present-day education often tends to develop mental fatigue, and can even create considerable frustration if not balanced by a recreational outlet. Everyone needs opportunities to relax mentally. The person who becomes engrossed in a satisfying recreational hobby such as dance can then see his problems with perspective and relaxed insight.

Development of confidence. Individual initiative and self-confidence are based upon previous individual successes. Although there are actually more opportunities for success today than there were in previous generations, that success often comes later in life because of job specialization and the extension of education. Thus many people lack initiative and self-confidence simply because they have had no opportunity for success.

Individual successes must be experienced early in life to build confidence as the child grows. Physical education activities present more opportunities for success than any other subject in school, and dance activities lead the entire field in such opportunities.

After experiencing several achievements, one naturally develops a sense of security and confidence. This in turn helps to eliminate such symptoms of insecurity as shyness and withdrawal, and helps the individual to become accepted in the group.

Self-evaluation. Dance movements offer one of the best activities an individual can use to determine his own capabilities. Through the development of coordination he can determine the difficulty of particular movements, and can also determine the status of his physical fitness.

Attitudes. One of the teacher's major tasks is to develop in his students wholesome attitudes that will carry over into adulthood. Dance can do much to help participants achieve acceptable attitudes. For example, it can give an individual an approved skill which will help him achieve social status—a status he might otherwise try to achieve by undesirable methods. It can also teach him consideration and sensitivity toward others. Each of us must learn early in life about the rights of others. This knowledge is not a sudden realization, of course; it comes with psychological growth. But each individual must have the opportunity to learn about and develop sensitivity for others, and dance, through its traditions and social demands, can offer this opportunity.

Recognition. Almost everyone requires recognition and approval for his achievements. Recognition is the refueling process that eliminates both mental and physical fatigue and usually spurs one on to greater effort. Approval involves a demonstration in the form of response. Dance supplies the participant both with recognition and with the response of approval, and through this response he learns to develop an artistic sense. This sense, combined with the many other values discussed in this chapter, contributes to the individual's development as an integrated mature personality.

3

Interpretation

of

Music

for

Dance

Music is generally defined as a combination of tones in a rhythmic sequence that forms an expressive composition. A piece of music can be compared with a story: each is made up of several parts and would be incomplete if any were omitted.

ORIGIN OF MUSIC

Man-made music probably began when prehistoric man first tried to imitate the musical sounds of nature with his voice. As he developed an appreciation for musical tones he was no doubt delighted by the twang of his bowstring, the singing of a thrown rock, the beating of sticks and rocks together, and the reverberative sounds from the whistles he made.

As time passed, primitive man learned to express his motor impulses by clapping his hands, stamping his feet, and striking objects together in rhythmic frequency. Eventually, he grouped musical and rhythmic sounds into a pattern to accompany dance festivities. Thus were developed the two prerequisites for music: tone and beat.

COMPONENTS OF MUSIC

Sound and movement are the two elements out of which all music is made. One cannot exist without the other, because sound takes place in time. Music is thus a combination of *tonal* and *temporal* components. Tonal components are pitch, timbre, dynamics, melody, and harmony. Temporal components are rhythm, tempo, and duration. The temporal aspects of music are the ones most important to students of dance.

Rhythm. Much in life is based on rhythm. For example, one can readily observe rhythm in speech, in the beat of the heart, in the tick of a clock. Rhythm affects both the mind and the body. It gives one feelings of balance, freedom, and power. It stimulates, it lulls, it brings on elation and excitement. It regulates the respiratory, excretory, and circulatory systems of the body. In fact, it sustains the whole human organism. Without it, the human mind and body would not be so durable as they are.

Understanding the fundamentals underlying rhythm is extremely important to the student of dance. Individuals vary in their ability to express rhythm bodily and in their sense of timing; but, with practice, everyone can improve his abilities in these skills so necessary to dance.

Those who have trouble in maintaining rhythm can practice such activities as jumping rope or dribbling a ball. Playing a musical instrument is, of course, an ideal way to improve rhythm.

Because dance is based on rhythm, students of dance must have a comprehensive understanding of the movements of sound. Sound is the prerequisite for musical rhythm, and rhythm is dependent upon the regularity of sound. In other words, rhythm is measured motion.

To chart this motion, an elaborate system of notation has been developed, and students of dance will find it helpful to become familiar at least with the terms and symbols concerned with rhythm.

Musical symbols. Specific symbols in writing, such as punctuation marks, were invented so that writers could express exact meanings. Composers of music have invented musical symbols for the same purpose. Instead of using words and punctuation marks, composers use notes, ties, dots, rests, and numerous other signs. The student of dance must understand the meanings and values of these symbols before he can specifically adapt a dance to music.

Our discussion must necessarily be limited to rhythmic notation. Symbols for pitch, other than notes themselves, will not be discussed. Such explanations can be found in music theory books.

Notes. A note specifies the length and the pitch of each musical tone. A *rest* specifies the length of a period of silence.

All notes are divisions of one note called a *whole note*. Each whole note (o) or whole rest (▬) gets four beats, counts, or pulsations. The whole note is divided into the following values: a *half note* (♩) or *half rest* (▬) gets two counts; a quarter note (♩) or quarter rest (𝄽) gets one count; two *eighth* notes (♪) or eighth rests (𝄾) get one count; and four *sixteenth* notes (♬) or sixteenth rests (𝄿) get one count. Occasionally *thirty-second* notes (♬) and *sixty-fourth* notes (♬) are also used.

A dot placed immediately after a note or rest increases the value of that note or rest by exactly one half its normal value. For example, a dotted half note (♩.) gets three counts rather than two.

Two or more eighth or sixteenth (or higher) notes can be joined together by a beam across the tops of the stems. The number of lines in the beam indicates the value of the notes.

         eighth notes   sixteenth notes

Sometimes three notes are grouped together with a beam and a 3 above it (♬). These are called *triplets,* and are performed in the same time normally used for two notes of the same value.

A *tie* is often used to connect two notes of the same pitch (♩ ♩). Unlike a beam, a tie connects the *counts* of the notes—that is, the count of the second note is added to that of the first note, creating one continuous tone.

The student of dance must know specifically how to count rhythms. This ability requires an exact knowledge of note values and their equivalent rests.

Music written in whole notes is not suitable for dance. In fact, it is not usual under any circumstances. Each whole note is assigned a count of four (1, 2, 3, 4) and dance steps usually occur on each of these counts. The optimum foot movements for most recreational dances are between 120 and 140 steps per minute, which means that there are between 120 and 140 quarter notes or their equivalent played in one minute.

When an exact speed is desired, a metronome marking is usually included in the music. For fairly accurate practice purposes, one might use the second hand of a watch. A clock with a good speed regulator can be set so that the second hand moves at the precise speed for normal quarter-note values.

Staffs, measures, and time signatures. The *staff,* which is used to show the pitch of each note, is composed of five horizontal lines and the four spaces between them. Staffs are divided into *bars* or *measures* by vertical lines. The number of counts in each measure is determined by the *time* or *meter signature.* This time signature is made up of two numbers placed one above the other at the beginning of the staff. The top number tells how many counts to give each measure and the bottom number tells what kind of beats are found in each measure. For example, music written in 4/4

Staff

Staff divided into measures

Time signature

Whole note   Whole rest

Counts: 1   2   3   4   1   2   3   4

Half notes   Half rests

1   2   3   4   1   2   3   4

Quarter notes   Quarter rests

1   2   3   4   1   2   3   4

Eighth notes   Eighth rests

1   &   2   &   3   &   4   &   1   &   2   &   3   &   4   &

Sixteenth notes   Sixteenth rests

1 - & - 2 - & - 3 - & - 4 - & -   1 - & - 2 - & - 3 - & - 4 - & -

The Tie

1 2 3 4   1   2   3   4

Triplets

1   2   3 -   - 4 -   -

Dotted notes

1 & 2 & 3 & - 4   &

time indicates that there are four quarter notes or their equivalent to each measure of music.

The following are the most common time signatures:

$\frac{4}{4}$ **C**   Four beats per measure. The symbol **C** is often used instead of 4/4 and is called "common time."

$\frac{3}{4}$ Three beats per measure.

$\frac{2}{4}$ $\frac{2}{2}$ **¢**   Two beats per measure. 2/2 time is also called "alla breve" and is abbreviated **¢**. 3/2 time is often counted as 2/2 time when the music is played at march tempo or faster.

$\frac{6}{8}$ Six beats per measure. 6/8 time is often called "compound duple rhythm" or "quick time." 3/8, 9/8, and 12/8 time receive the same counts as 6/8 time, and 2/2 time is counted as 6/8 when played slowly.

Meter. The number of beats and the pattern of *accents* in a measure of music is the meter. Accents may be described as additional emphasis or stress on certain beats. It is impossible to determine meter without the existence of at least two accented beats, because without accents one cannot define the start and finish of a measure. For example, meter does not exist in the ticking of a clock, because no accented beat occurs.

Meters having two pulse beats in a measure of music are called *duple meters.* Those having three beats are called *triple meters.* Compound meters are those having four, five, six, or seven pulse beats per measure. When accents fall naturally at the beginning of each measure, and in a series of equal measures, they are said to be *regular.* When accents are placed on a normally unaccented or weaker part of the measure, the meter is called *syncopated.*

Occasionally one finds a piece of music whose accented beat within a consistent meter varies from measure to measure. However, in most instances, the first beat of each measure receives the accent. Sometimes, for special effects, the meter itself might vary from measure to measure.

Counterpoint is the existence of two or more complimentary melodies occurring simultaneously. A *round* is an example of a type of counterpoint.

Resultant rhythm occurs when two meters are performed simultaneously. For example, one rhythm might be counted in 2/4 and another, played at the same time, might be counted in 3/4. It would take six beats to complete this particular resultant pattern.

Dances are performed in counterpoint or resultant rhythm when one person or group is moving to one melody or rhythm, and another person or group is moving to the second melody or rhythm. This type of dance takes considerable concentration, and is another example of why students of dance must understand rhythm and meter.

Rhythm patterns. Rhythm usually falls into one of three patterns: *even, uneven,* or *broken.* Each pattern requires different dance steps. The determination of which rhythm type a particular musical selection contains depends on a combination of melodic notation and rhythmic base in the selection.

Even rhythm, the simplest type, occurs when the melody or the pattern of beats is identical to the meter or underlying beat. Movements such as walking, running, hopping, jumping, and leaping, and the steps used in the waltz and the schottische, are best executed to even rhythm.

Example:

4 ♩ ♩ ♩ ♩   melody pattern

4 ___ ___ ___ ___   underlying beat

Uneven rhythm is a combination of slow and quick beats. The gallop, polka, skip, and slide work best to this kind of rhythm.

Example:

4 ♩ ♩ ♩   melody pattern

4 ___ ___ ___ ___   underlying beat

Broken rhythm occurs in a combination of slow and quick beats where the rhythm pattern extends into a second measure. Some fox trot and swing music contains this type of rhythm.

Example:

4 ♩ ♩ | ♫   melody pattern

4 __ __ | __ __ underlying beat

Once the student understands these basic rhythm patterns, he will be able to analyze the rhythm requirements of most pieces of music. The dance movements themselves will then become easier to perform.

Phrasing. A musical phrase usually consists of from two to eight measures and expresses a complete musical thought. A group of phrases completes a piece of music just as a group of paragraphs completes a story.

Phrases are frequently repeated, just as the chorus or refrain of a song is repeated after each stanza. In most dances, when a phrase of music is repeated, so is the dance step.

Often, to avoid unnecessary repetition in musical notation, repeat signs are used. The repeat sign indicates to the performer that he is to return to the beginning or to the previous sign and perform the phrase again.

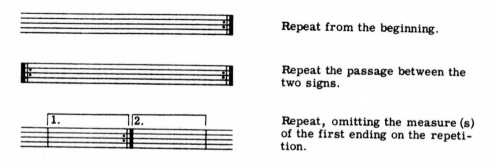

Repeat from the beginning.

Repeat the passage between the two signs.

Repeat, omitting the measure (s) of the first ending on the repetition.

Tempo. *Tempo* refers to the speed at which a piece of music is performed. Circumstances other than the music itself frequently dictate how fast a piece of music should be played. Some instructors prefer to slow down the music when basic or complicated steps are being learned. At other times, a faster tempo than the music indicates may be desired. Also, dances are sometimes performed at double or half time—that is, the tempo of the steps is twice as fast or half as fast as the established count or beat.

Although the tempo may be varied to suit special conditions, the following metronomic quarter-note tempos are standard for the indicated dances.

two-step (6/8 time)	100–116 beats per minute
polka (2/4 time)	100–116
march (4/4 time)	116–136
schottische (4/4 time)	136–148
waltz (3/4 time):	
fast	90–98
moderate	54–72
slow	44–52

Musical terms. Instructions for interpretation are often written on the music itself. The following is a list of musical terms with which students of dance should be familiar in order to create steps that portray the feelings intended by the music.

accelerando: increasing in tempo
adagio: slowly, smoothly
agitato: in a hurry, restless, excited
allegro: briskly, quickly .
andante: moderately, gracefully
animato: lively, animated
appassionato: with great feeling
brillante: bright, sparkling, brilliant
coda: the final summary, or climax of the whole composition
crescendo: an increase in loudness
decrescendo: gradual decrease in loudness
finale: the ending
forte: strong and loud
grandioso: in a grand or noble manner
largo: hesitatingly, solemnly
legato: in a graceful and smooth manner
lento: slowly, smoothly
maestoso: dignified, stately, majestic
mezzo: medium
piano: soft
presto: hurriedly, very fast
rallentando: a slow decrease in time
scherzo: lively and gay, with rapid rhythm
staccato: clear and distinct tones, separate from each other
tremolo: quivering or trembling
vibrante: pulsing, vigorous
vivace: lively, very fast

4

Teaching

Techniques

and

Facilities

In the learning of any subject it is essential that the teacher be well prepared, use effective teaching methods, and have adequate equipment and facilities. Experienced dance teachers have developed their own ideas about procedures, equipment, and so on. Therefore, this chapter is directed to the beginning teacher.

TEACHING TECHNIQUES

It seems senseless to include a long list of "do's and dont's" that would cover every situation that the beginning teacher might encounter. Instead, listed below are some of the techniques that I have found essential for the development of sustained interest in dance activities.

1. First, the teacher must be capable of executing rhythmical movements and must be highly enthusiastic about dance. Nothing is more deadly than a dance class conducted by an uncoordinated or uninspired teacher.

2. The teacher must know his materials. He should seldom refer to written materials while actually teaching. If he finds teaching aids necessary, they should be placed on cue cards.

3. Dance by its very nature is social. Consequently, it is essential that the teacher instill in students a desire to learn. At the same time the students should thoroughly enjoy each dance experience. This requires a balance between control and relaxation. The students should be expected to give complete attention to all instructions. Still, the teacher should allow conversational periods throughout all dance activities. This can easily be done by having frequent unstructured reviews of previously taught dances.

4. Some teachers prefer to have the students in straight lines, while others prefer squares or circles for teaching purposes. I prefer the broken circle or horseshoe formation, with the teacher at the broken end of the formation. If the teacher faces the class while demonstrating a basic movement, he should use opposite footwork for himself. This prevents considerable class confusion.

5. Difficult dances should be taught in parts—one or two steps today, other steps later.

6. When possible the students should learn the dance at its proper performance tempo.

7. Most teachers are guilty of talking too much and teaching too slowly. Students are capable of assimilating materials faster than is generally believed. Also, the class or dance club should not be held back because two or three students are having difficulty.

8. When there are more than twenty students in the class or club, ninety per cent of the instructional time should be spent in group instruction, *not* individual instruction.

9. Frequent changing of partners generally improves total class morale.

10. The teacher should give all instructions in a clear, distinct, friendly tone. The students should be able to understand directions quickly and easily.

11. Most teachers find that it is advantageous occasionally to include humorous dances in the program.

12. The teacher should not include dances or dance steps that are beyond the students' ability to learn.

13. When possible, lead-up dances should be used to facilitate learning.

14. General historical background, costumes, and appropriate accompaniment add interest to dance instruction.

15. Opportunities for dance exhibitions increase the determination to master skills. This is especially true with young people.

16. Some teachers like to use the blackboard to write the name of the dance, nationality, basic steps, formation, and so on. I seldom use this technique, because I believe it slows down the progress of the class.

17. I prefer to demonstrate and teach the basic steps, and then get the class in the proper formation and underway. The students are always eager to begin dancing. Historical, cultural, and general background information is important but should be supplemental and added from time to time as the dance is reviewed.

18. I prefer to teach the dance in tempo, cuing the beginning of the dance and each new step. All cues should be eliminated at the earliest possible time when dances are being reviewed.

19. I prefer to teach the dance in the exact order in which it is supposed to be performed. This way the students find it easier to remember the arrangement of steps and sequences.

20. Above all, the teacher should be able to analyze each step and movement, present it clearly, and never over-challenge the class.

These are just a few of the many fundamentals and techniques used by an experienced teacher in dance. Each instructor should of course add to this list the techniques that he finds successful.

FACILITIES

Specially equipped rooms are desirable for dance classes. Rooms should be adequately decorated, properly ventilated, and acoustically constructed. The floors should not be too slippery or sticky.

Many excellent kinds of equipment are available for the teaching of dance. Teachers generally develop some preference of record players, accompaniment, tape recorders, records, costumes, and props in general. Most major brands of recording equipment give satisfactory performance if properly used.

5

Fundamental

Dance

Movements

The teacher of dance must know what note values are best for fundamental foot and body movements. In this chapter we will discuss basic body movements as they relate to rhythmical patterns.

Walking. Walking is a continuous process in which one foot pushes the body forward while the other foot goes forward to prevent the body from falling. One foot is thus always on the ground, and the weight is transferred smoothly from the heel to the ball of the foot.

Many people find it difficult to walk in cadence. This activity should be one of the first taught in elementary school. A steady, even rhythm in 4/4 time is best for walking in cadence.

Recommended exercises for walking to music:

1. Practice clapping hands to the music, accenting the primary and secondary beats.

2. Practice walking in place (marking time), making sure that the left foot makes contact with the floor on the accented beat. Practice raising the knees at first high and then not so high. Stay with the music. Stand tall but not rigid.

3. Practice making noise with the feet (stamping). Next, try walking noiselessly while at the same time keeping step with the music.

4. Walk around the room, at first noisily and then very softly. Let the arms swing freely, be as tall as possible, keep the eyes straight ahead, and never look down.

5. Take a step to the side and then draw the other foot alongside. Reverse this procedure and move in the opposite direction.

6. Practice walking while swinging the arms forward and backward diagonally across the body. Try alternate and parallel arm movements while walking.

7. Walk sideways with the feet crossing over each other, first in front and then in back. This step is known as the *grapevine step.*

8. Practice the grapevine step on tiptoes.

9. Practice walking half as fast as the musical tempo and then twice as fast as the tempo.

10. Practice walking to "Green Sleeves" (RCA Victor LPM 1624) and "Red River Valley" (Folk Dancer 3013A).

Running. The best music to accompany running is a fast even rhythm in 4/4 time. The music is usually written in eighth notes.

Running is faster than walking and both feet leave the ground at the same time.

Recommended exercises for running to music:

1. Clap the hands in time to the music, accenting the heavy beats.

2. Practice running in place, letting the left foot strike the floor on the heavy beat of the music. Keep the body as tall as possible while running.

3. Practice running to slow music. The height of the stride is increased as the music gets slower. Keep the eyes focused at a distance while running.

4. With faster music, shorten the step and lower the stride.

5. Experiment with different arm movements while running.

6. Try the grapevine step while running. Step sideways with the left foot, in front with the right, sideways with the left, and in back with the right. Repeat these movements.

7. A simple dance in which the running steps are basic is the Russian "Troika" (Folk Dancer MH 1059).

Hopping. The best music for hopping is an even rhythm in 4/4 time (quarter notes). In hopping, a person jumps and lands on the ball of the same foot. The knee should be bent to prevent jarring when landing.

Recommended exercises for hopping to music:

1. Practice clapping hands to the music, accenting the beat.
2. Practice hopping in place, eight times on one foot and then eight times on the other.
3. Practice hopping with the free foot extended first in front and then in back.
4. Practice doing a heel-toe step with the free foot. Change weight, using the opposite foot to hop on without losing time.
5. Practice advancing, retreating, and turning around while hopping.
6. Two easy dances in which there is ample opportunity to practice the hop step are "Highland Schottische" (RCA Victor 45-6179) and "Patty Cake Polka" (Folkraft F1177A).

Jumping. Another basic movement in dance is the jump. It is best practiced with an even rhythm in 4/4 time (quarter notes). Unlike hopping, jumping requires landing on both feet at the same time, although the jump may be started on one foot. The take-off and landing should be on the balls of the feet, with knees bent to absorb shock.

Recommended exercises for jumping:

1. Clap hands to the music, accenting the beat.
2. Jump in place (keeping the knees relaxed), turn in place, advance, retreat, and jump sideways.
3. Practice jumping as high as possible, keeping time with the music.
4. Practice fast and slow jumps.
5. Experiment with foot and arm movements while jumping. Raise knees high in front; raise heels as high in back as possible. Jump while holding the arms in various positions.
6. Three easy dances in which jump steps occur are the Mexican "La Raspa" (Columbia 6190X), the Swedish "Bleking" (RCA Victor 45-6169), and the French "La Robe Du Chat" (Folkraft F1105).

Leaping. Leaping is one of the most exhilarating motor movements. It is executed by transferring the weight from one foot to the other while running with long strides. It is similar to a high run. The best music has an even rhythm in 4/4 time (quarter notes).

Recommended exercises for leaping:

1. Practice clapping the hands in time to the music.
2. Practice taking as long a step as possible.
3. Practice taking three running steps and then a leap, such as left, right, left, leap right. Then start on the right foot and execute the same movements. Also, take two steps and then leap. This will bring about leaps on alternate feet.
4. Do a series of fast, low, running leaps with no steps in between. Then practice high bounding leaps.
5. Take several running steps and then make a high leap.

6. Recommended folk dances that have a leap in the routine are the Jewish "Misirlou" (RCA Victor 45-5047), the Mexican "Mi Pecosita" (ASP 102B), the Russian "Hopak" (Kismet 5116), and the Israeli "Harmonica" (Folkraft F1108A).

Skipping. Skipping is done best to an uneven rhythm in 2/4 time. Skipping is difficult for some people. It involves taking a long step and then hopping on the same foot. It is easier to learn how to skip on one foot and take a walking step with the other.

Recommended exercises for skipping:
   1. First, clap the musical beat.
   2. Take slow step-hops in place and then gradually increase the tempo.
   3. Practice taking walking steps with the right foot and step-hops with the left foot. Then reverse this procedure, doing the step-hops with the right foot and the walking steps with the left foot.
   4. Eliminate the walking steps, taking step-hops with each foot in turn.
   5. Recommended folk dances in which the skip step or step-hop may be used are the German "Rheinländer for Three" (Folk Dancer 1050B), the Mexican "Chihuahua" (Windsor A754), the Mexican "La Costilla" (Windsor 752), and the American "Skip to My Lou" (Folkraft 1192).

Sliding. Sliding is the easiest of the uneven movements. It is executed by taking a sideward step, drawing up the other foot, and then quickly changing the weight from one foot to the other. The music is usually written in 2/4 time, using dotted eighth and sixteenth notes.

Recommended exercises for sliding:
   1. Clap in time to the music.
   2. Using different tempos, practice sliding movements to the left, to the right, forward, and backward. In the latter two movements, the trailing foot should never pass the forward foot.
   3. Recommended folk dances in which the sliding step is used are the German "Kinderpolka" (RCA Victor 45-6179), the Swedish "Carrousel" (45-6179), and the Hungarian "Cshebogar" (45-6182).

Galloping. The gallop is similar to the slide except that both feet are off the floor at the same time. The forward foot takes a long step and the back foot a short step. The gallop is just as easy as the slide. Music in 2/4 time, as for the slide and skip, supplies the most satisfactory accompaniment.

Recommended exercises for the gallop:
   1. Clap out the rhythm.
   2. Practice doing the step in place, raising the knee of the first foot higher than the other. Then reverse the footwork.

3. Gallop around the room, leading with first one foot for a few steps and then the other.

4. Recommended dances that have related steps are "Sur Le Bord De La Riviere" (Folkraft 1105), "Cotton Eyed Joe" (Folkraft 1035), and "Patty Cake Polka" (Folkraft F1260A&B).

Additional fundamentals. Other basic dance fundamentals that should be practiced to music are bending and stretching, swinging and swaying, pushing and pulling, striking and dodging, turning and twisting, shaking and beating, and rising and falling. The ability to perform these fundamentals rhythmically increases one's skill in performing any type of dance.

6

Elementary

Folk

Dances

The dances described in this chapter are composed of simple steps and elementary routines. They are arranged according to their degree of difficulty to perform. The dances, which are easy to learn and fun to do, include basic fundamental movements essential for advanced work in dance.

Each of the dances in this chapter can be taught in a few minutes. These dances should be taught before any analysis is made of their individual movements. The beginning student learns more quickly by observation and imitation than by analysis and interpretation. The teacher should demonstrate briefly and then have the student imitate the movements.

The student will accomplish most when his interest is high. The dances should be taught with enthusiasm, which is contagious and will stimulate greater participation.

The teacher must know exactly how he is going to teach each dance. He should coordinate the steps with the music before class time, and should never try to work out steps while the class is in progress. He should be sure he knows the dance well, and should never read the instructions while teaching.

HOKEY POKEY (American)

Type: Traditional play-party dance. Teaches right and left hand and foot movements. Tends to aid in eliminating shyness and self-consciousness.
Reference and music: Record: MacGregor 699A. (2/4 time.)
Formation: Single circle, all dancers facing the center.
Basic steps: Dancers move parts of their bodies in and out of the circle as the caller determines.

A. "You put your right foot IN,
   You put your right foot OUT,
   You put your right foot IN,
   Then you shake it all about.
   You do the Hokey-Pokey,
   And you turn yourself around,
   That's what it's all about."
B. Left foot (Repeat first verse, substituting the words indicated)
C. Right arm
D. Left arm
E. Right elbow
F. Left elbow
G. Head
H. Right hip
 I. Left hip
 J. Whole self
K. Back side

BLEKING (Swedish)

Type: Couple dance. Develops timing and coordination. This dance is named after a Swedish province.
Reference: Van Hagen, p. 502.
Music: Records: RCA Victor 45-6169, 20989, LPM-1622; Folkraft 1188. Piano score: La Salle.* (2/4 time.)
Formation: Single circle, partners facing each other with both hands joined.
Basic step: Bleking step.

* See the Bibliography at the end of this book for full information.

Measures:

1　Hop with right heel forward and left toe back; hop with left heel forward and right toe back.

2　Repeat the step with three quick changes—left, right, left.

3–8　Repeat measures 1 and 2 three more times.

9–16　Turn partner with step-hops starting on boy's left foot and girl's right foot, holding hands with partner, arms extended sideward.

Repeat the dance from beginning.

GAY MUSICIAN (French)

Type: Play-party dance.
Source and music: Record: Folkraft * 1185. (2/4 time.)
Formation: Single circle, all dancers facing the center.
Basic steps: Walk, skip.
Measures:

SONG

1–4　"I am a gay musician, from Flanders I have come,

5–8　I can play sweet music, upon my little drum.

9–10　D-rr-r-um, dum dum, d-rr-r-um, dum dum,

11–12　D-rr-r-um, dum dum, d-rr-r-um, dum dum,

13–16　Skipping and playing, everywhere straying,

17–18　D-rr-r-um, dum dum, d-rr-r-um, dum dum,

19–20　D-rr-r-um, dum dum, dum dee."

(For Flanders, substitute name of your home town.)

ACTION

1–8　All face and walk counterclockwise singing.

9–10　Face center and pantomime the playing of an instrument.

13–16　Face and skip counterclockwise singing.

17–20　Face center and pantomime the playing of an instrument.

KINDERPOLKA (German)

Type: Children's polka; couple dance. Can be used as a mixer when the boy moves forward to the next girl. Teaches draw step, timing, and an elementary rhythmic pattern.

Reference and music: Records: RCA Victor 45-6179, LPM-1625; Folkraft 1187. Piano score: Van Hagen, p. 437. (2/4 time.)

Formation: Single circle, partners facing with hands joined. Arms extended sideways, shoulder high. Boys face counterclockwise, girls face clockwise. (Boys' steps are described below: girls do a counterstep.)

Basic steps: Draw step, stamps, claps, turns.

* Instructions used by permission of Folkraft Record Company.

Single circle, partners facing.

Measures:

PART I

1–2 *Draw—draw:* take two draw steps toward the center (step-close, step-close). *Stamp-stamp-stamp:* take three steps in place.

3–4 *Draw—draw:* take two draw steps to original place; *stamp-stamp-stamp:* take three steps in place.

5–8 Repeat all of Part I.

PART II

9–10 (1) *Slap thighs,* (2) *clap own hands,* (3) *clap partner's hands three times.*

11–12 Repeat Part II.

PART III

13–14 *Right finger shake:* place right heel forward and shake right forefinger at partner three times; hold left hand under right elbow. Repeat with left heel and forefinger.

15–16 *Turn in place:* two steps; *Stamp-stamp-stamp:* take three steps in place.

Repeat from beginning.

TERSCHELLING REEL NO. 1 (Dutch)

Type: Dutch "flip." Teaches draw steps and turns with jump steps.
Source: As performed at the U.S.C. Dance Workshop.
Music: Record: Columbia DB-1798. (4/4 time.)
Formation: Couples in social dance position, double circle. (Boys' steps are described; girls do a counterstep; boys start on left feet, girls on right.)
Basic steps: Draw steps, jumps, and turns in two steps.
Measures:

1–2 Four bouncy step-close steps (left, close right, left) in line of direction. The joined hands are pointed forward with elbows straight.

3–4 Four bouncy step-close steps in reverse line of direction, dancers still retaining the same positions.

5–6 Two step-close steps in line of direction; two step-close steps in reverse line of direction.

7–8 Turn away from partner (boy left, girl right) in two steps. Face partner: (1) jump with feet together; (2) jump with feet apart; (3) jump with feet together.

Repeat entire dance.

THE BRAID—PLETYONKA (Russian)

Type: Round dance mixer.
Source and music: Record: Folkraft * 1169. (2/4 time.)
Formation: Double circle with partners facing. Girls are in inner circle, backs to center, with hands on hips, elbows forward, and left foot free. Boys' arms are folded in front of chests.
Basic steps: Walk, two-steps.
Measures:

1 Hop on right foot; touch left toe to side with toe turned in and heel up; look at partner over left shoulder (counts 1 and). Hop on right foot and extend left foot forward, turning to face partner (2 and).

2 Hop on left foot; touch right toe to side with toe turned in and heel up; look at partner over right shoulder (1 and). Hop on left foot and extend right foot forward, turning to face partner (2 and).

3–4 Repeat pattern of measures 1 and 2.

5–8 Hook right elbows with partner, raising left hands high, and swing clockwise one and three-quarter times around with eight running steps. Finish in a single circle, boys facing out, girls facing in, keeping right elbows linked; hook left elbows with neighbor.

9–14 Circle clockwise with six two-steps, a polka step, or twelve running steps; keep elbows linked, and look over left shoulder at new partner.

15–16 Release right arms and, keeping left arms linked, swing one-quarter way around in four steps to finish in the original position but facing a new partner.

* Instructions used by permission of Folkraft Record Company.

BUNNY HOP (American)

Type: Play-party dance. Teaches group coordination.
Reference and music: Record: MacGregor 699. (4/4 time.)
Formation: Single line, alternating boy and girl.
Basic steps: Side kick, jump, foot change of weight.
Measures:

1–2 Slight hop on right foot; extend left foot out to side hop; bring left back.
Repeat same movement, changing weight on last step.
3–4 Slight hop on left foot; extend right foot out; bring right foot back.
Repeat same movements. End with feet together.
5 Jump on both feet forward.
6 Jump backward.
7–8 Jump three times forward.
Repeat from beginning.

HORA (Israeli)

Type: Round dance. One of the most popular folk dances in the Balkan countries. It is the national dance of Israel.
Source: As performed by international students at U.S.C.
Music: Records: Folkraft F1110B; Folkraft 1116A; RCA Victor LPM-1623; Educational Dance Recordings FD-2. (2/4 time.)
Formation: Closed circle. Hands on shoulders of persons on each side.
Basic step: Side step.
Measures:

Counts
1 1: Place left foot to left.
   2: Place right foot behind left.
2 1: Step sideward on left foot to left.
   2: Swing right foot across in front of left.
3 1. Step sideward on right foot to right.
   2: Swing left foot across in front of right.
Repeat measures 1–3 throughout dance.

GREEN SLEEVES (English)

Type: Spirited marching country dance. Teaches walking to music.
Source: Los Angeles City Schools Institute Outline.
Music: Records: RCA Victor 45-1624; Educational Dance Recordings FD-1. (2/4 time.)
Formation: Double circle, partners side by side facing counterclockwise, girl on the right, inside hands joined. Couples number off in twos.
Basic steps: Walk, right- and left-hand star, arch.

Measures:

PART I

1–8 *Walk:* starting on left foot, all walk forward sixteen steps.

PART II

9–12 *Right-hand star:* first couple turns back to face second couple, making a four-hand, right-hand star clockwise in eight steps.

13–16 *Left-hand star:* both couples turn half-right, making a left-hand star counterclockwise in eight steps.

PART III

17–18 *Two over one:* second couple forms arch with inside hands, walks forward four steps as first couple backs under the arch in four steps.

19–20 *One over two:* repeat with first couple forming arch for second couple.

21–24 Repeat measures 17–20.

Single circle facing center.

SEVEN JUMPS (Danish)

Type: Vigorous acrobatic dance. No false moves are permitted during the dance. Dancers who make mistakes must pay penalties. Teaches balance.

References: RCA Victor recording; Van Hagen, p. 519.

Elementary Folk Dances   55

SEVEN JUMPS

Moderately

Arranged by Louise Hall

Continue thus seven times, adding a measure each time.

*Indicates that the notes are held various lengths of time (not in tempo).

Music: Record: RCA Victor LPM-1623. Piano score: See page 57. (2/4 time.)

Formation: Single circle, all dancers facing center and holding hands.

Basic steps: Sideward skip, balance.

Measures:

1–8   Skip sideward seven times, moving clockwise; then jump and bring feet together on measure 8.

9–16   Jump and repeat skips, moving counterclockwise.

17(a) Raise right foot; release hands and place them on hips.

18   Replace foot on ground. Remain motionless.

1–18   Repeat as before.

17(b) Raise left foot.

18   Replace left foot. Stand motionless.

1–18   Repeat all.

Each time measure 17 is reached, repeat each movement performed previously and then add another movement, in the order below. Return to original skip after performing each set of movements.

17(c) Kneel down on right knee.

17(d) Kneel down on left knee.

17(e) Bend right elbow and rest head on fist.

17(f) Bend left elbow and rest head on fist.

17(g) Place hands back of head.

ALL-AMERICAN PROMENADE (American)

Type: Basic American folk dance. Teaches marching steps.

Reference and music: Records: Windsor A7S4; Windsor 7605. (4/4 time.)

Formation: Double circle, boys on inside. Couples face counterclockwise. Begin on boy's left foot, girl's right.

Basic step: Walk.

Measures:

1–4   Holding inside hands and starting on outside foot, walk four steps counterclockwise, turning towards partner on last step to end with backs in line of direction.

5–8   Walk four steps in line of direction, backing up. End up in original starting position.

9–10   Balance together; balance apart.

11–12 Change sides in three steps and point foot. Girl crosses in front of boy.

13–14 Balance together; balance apart (repeat action of measures 9–10 in partner's place).

15–16 In four walking steps boy moves forward to next girl while girl twirls clockwise.

MAKEDONKA (Macedonian)

Type: Medium-speed round dance. Macedonian dances are usually in slow tempo and resemble Greek and Serbian dances. Teaches slow foot movements.

Source: Los Angeles City Schools Institute Outline.
Music: Records: Balkan 547; Stanchel 1022.
Formation: Broken circle, dancers holding hands.
Basic step: Kolo (fast and slow steps).
Measures:

1 *Side-behind-side* (R-L-R): start with a long slow step on the right foot, bring the left foot quickly from behind, and take a quick right step to the side.

2 *Front-side-front* (L-R-L): take a long step on the left foot in front of the right, a quick right in line of direction, and a quick left in front of the right.

3 *In-two-three* (R-L-R): take a slow right, a quick left, and a quick right step toward center of circle.

4 *Out-two-three* (L-R-L): back out three steps with a slow left and two quick right and left steps. The count throughout the dance is slow-quick-quick.

Repeat measures 1–4 throughout the dance.

CARROUSEL (Swedish)

Type: Singing play-party dance. Title is derived from the acceleration that takes place in Part II. Teaches slow and fast side steps.
Source: Traditional.
Music: Records: RCA Victor 45-6179, 20432; Folkraft 1183. (4/4 time.)
Formation: Double circle, all dancers facing center. Girls on inside holding hands with girls on either side. Boys stand behind and place hands on partners' shoulders.
Basic step: Side-sliding step (draw step).
Measures:

PART I

1–4 Sixteen sliding steps (draw steps) clockwise to the left. Stamp on last three steps. (Step left foot to side, close right foot to left, repeat fifteen times.)

PART II

5–8 As the tempo increases, speed up so that the slide becomes a galop. All sing:
"Little children young and gay, Carrousel is running.
It will run till evening. Little ones a nickel,
Big ones a dime. Hurry up, get a mate
Or you'll surely be too late."

9–12 *(faster)*
"Ha ha ha! Happy are we,
Anderson and Henderson and Peterson and me."

Begin the dance again by starting in the opposite direction.

BINGO (American)

Type: Play-party dance. Teaches marching, singing, and grand right and left.
Reference: Handy Play Party Book.
Music: Record: RCA Victor 45-6172. (4/4 time.)
Formation: Double circle; boys are on inside, facing counterclockwise. Couples hold hands. All start on left foot.
Basic step: Walk.
Measures:
A. 1–8 Walk sixteen steps counterclockwise. All sing:
"A big black dog sat on the back porch,
And Bingo was his name,
A big black dog sat on the back porch,
And Bingo was his name."
B. 1–8 All join hands, girls on boys' right, and circle counterclockwise.
"B-I-N-G-O, B-I-N-G-O, B-I-N-G-O,
And Bingo was his name."
C. 1–8 Partners face (girls face clockwise, boys counterclockwise) and start grand right and left, joining hands with a different person on each spelled-out letter.
"B-I-N-G-O"
The couples meeting on "O" (the fifth change) join right elbows and turn around once before starting again from the beginning.

KARAPYET (Russian)

Type: Couple two-step. Karapyet refers to an old Russian drinking song.
Source: As performed at the U.S.C. Dance Workshop, 1956; developed from Folkraft Records outline.
Music: Records: Folkraft 1169; Folk Dancer MH-1058; Educational Dance Recordings FD-4. (2/4 time.)
Formation: Couples in open ballroom position facing counterclockwise. Start on outside foot.
Basic steps: Walk, two-step.
Measures:

PART I

1–2 Toe forward and back. Point toe of outside foot forward; then point it back.
3–4 Walk two three counterclockwise. Take three walking steps forward, starting on outside foot. Turn sharply on last beat without changing hold.
5–8 Repeat clockwise. Finish facing counterclockwise.

PART II

1–2 Balance toward and away from partner.

3–4 Turn, drop hands, turn forward and around counterclockwise in four steps.

5–8 Repeat measures 1–4.

PART III

1–2 Walk two three hop counterclockwise.

3–4 Walk two three hop clockwise.

5–8 Two-steps. Take four turning two-steps clockwise, advancing counterclockwise.

ALUNELUL (Rumanian)

Type: Round dance. Title means "little hazelnut." Teaches group coordination.

Source: As performed at the U.S.C. Dance Workshop, 1956.

Music: Records: Folk Dancer MH-1120; Elektra EKL-206. (2/4 time.)

Formation: Closed circle. Arms on shoulders.

Basic steps: Fast side step and kick.

Measures:

1–4 All move five steps to right starting with right foot, left foot going behind; then stamp twice with left heel.

5–8 Repeat measures 1–4, moving to the left with opposite foot work.

9–10 Move right three steps (right, left, right; left foot going behind right); stamp left heel.

11–12 Move left three steps, using opposite foot work; stamp right heel.

13–16 In place: step right, stamp left; step left, stamp right; step right, stamp left twice.

17–20 Repeat measures 13–16, using opposite footwork.

Repeat measures 13–20.

INDIAN RAIN DANCE (American)

Type: Round dance. Teaches basic toe-heel steps.

Reference and music: Record: Folkraft F1192B and accompanying description by Olga Kulbitsky. (4/4 time.)

Formation: Single circle facing center. Arms folded in front of chest.

Basic step: Toe-heel step.

Measures:

PART I

1–4 *Bow-up, bow-up, bow-up, bow-up.* Bend forward, extending arms outward and upward (counts 1–2). Return to starting position with arms folded (counts 3–4). Repeat this pattern four times.

5–6 *Walk two three four.* Walk toward center four steps raising arms slowly, reaching peak height on last count.

7–8 *Back two three four.* Return to starting position.

9–12 *Raise arms upward four times.* Look up each time.

13–16 *Toe-heel.* Turn right in small circle with eight toe-heel steps.

PART II

1–4 *Look, look, look, look.* Shade eyes with hand and step right; bring foot back, step left (still shading eyes). Repeat entire pattern four times.

5–8 *Listen, listen, listen, listen.* Repeat measures 1–4, cupping hands over ears. Repeat pattern four times.

9–12 *Toe-heel.* Turn right with eight toe-heel steps.

13–16 Turn left with eight toe-heel steps.

PART III

1 *Jump* (counts 1–2); land (counts 3–4).

2 *"Woo, Woo, Woo."* Do Indian call three times.

3–4 Repeat measures 1–2.

5–6 *Toe-heel.* Take four toe-heel steps forward, raising arms.

7–8 *Back.* Take four toe-heel steps backward, arms in place.

9–16 Repeat measures 1–8.

Costumes for Indian Rain Dance.

THE WHEAT (Czechoslovakian)

Type: Three-person dance. Representative of occupational folk dances. Teaches accented steps.

Reference and music: Record: RCA Victor LPM-1625. Piano score: *Handy Play Party Book,* p. 115. (2/4 time.)

Formation: Groups of three, a boy between two girls or vice versa. Link arms three abreast.

Basic steps: Walk, skip.

Measures:

1–8   Beginning on left feet, the three dancers walk forward sixteen steps.

9–12 Center person hooks right arm with person on his right. The two dancers turn twice around with eight skipping steps.

13–16 Center person hooks left arm with person on his left. These two turn twice around with eight skipping steps.

Repeat measures 1–16.

VERSE

1

From the feast there came a farmer,
On his back a bag of bran,
And the bad boys shouted at him,
"Let those pigeons out, old man."

2

"Let those pigeons out, old man,
Let those pigeons out, old man,"
And the bad boys shouted at him,
"Let those pigeons out, old man."

TROIKA (Russian)

Type: Three-person dance. Representative of folkways in the time when coaches were as common as taxis are today. Teaches fast running steps to music.

Source: As performed at the U.S.C. Dance Workshop.

Music: Records: Folk Dancer MH-1059; Educational Dance Recordings FD-2. Piano score: Van Hagen, p. 616. (2/4 time.)

Formation: Groups of three, a boy between two girls. The coachman is the center person; the outside two are ponies. Coachman holds ponies by inside hands.

Basic step: Running step.

Measures:

1–4   Starting with right foot, all run sixteen steps forward, taking two steps to each beat.

5–8   Pony on left runs around the other two in sixteen steps. Coachman and pony on right mark time, holding hands throughout dance.

9–12 The two ponies join outside hands, each group of three thus forming a circle. Each group takes fourteen running steps in a circle to the left and then stamps twice.

13–14 All take eight running steps in a circle to the right.

15–16 The two ponies raise their joined hands, forming an arch, and swing the coachman forward to the group in front of them.

VERSE

Hear the merry sleigh bells ringing,
See the horses stepping high.
See how they are prancing,

See how they are dancing,
Underneath the blue and wintry sky.
Hi, hi, hi and ho, ho, ho,
As over the hill and dale we go.

SHOEMAKER'S DANCE (Danish)

Type: Round dance. An occupational dance depicting the shoemaker at work in ancient days.
Reference: Van Hagen, p. 520.
Music: Records: RCA Victor 20450; RCA Victor LPM-1624; Folkraft 1187. (2/4 time.)
Formation: Double circle, partners facing, boys on inside of circle. Hands on hips.
Basic step: Polka or skip.
Measures:

1	Revolve fists around each other as if winding thread.
2	Reverse first movement.
3	Pull fists away from each other twice as if breaking the thread.
4	Pound one fist on the other three times as if driving pegs.
5–8	Repeat measures 1–4.
9–16	Face-to-face and back-to-back polka, or shoulder-waist polka, or skip, in a circle counterclockwise. Boys begin on left feet, girls on right.

Repeat from beginning.

KIIGADE KAAGADI (Estonian)

Type: Couple swing dance.
Source: As performed at the U.S.C. Dance Workshop, 1958.
Music: Record: Recorded Sound Ltd. RSL-911.
Formation: Couples in open position, facing clockwise, holding inside hands while outside hands swing freely. Boys start on left feet, girls on right.
Basic steps: Step-hop, face-to-face, back-to-back polka.
Measures:

1–2	Couples take four step-hops clockwise, starting on outside feet (boy's left foot, girls right). Finish by turning inward and changing hands.
3–4	Repeat step-hops counterclockwise, starting on inside foot.
5–8	Repeat measures 1–4.
9	Couples stand face to face, both hands joined. Boys' steps are described; girls do counterpart. Step sideways to the left, close with the right, take another side step left, and turn back to back, letting go with left hand and joining hands again when back to back.
10	While back to back, take a side step right, close with the left, take another side step right, hop on the right, and turn to face each other, taking shoulder-waist hold.
11–12	Take three step-hops, turning clockwise and finishing with a small jump, landing on both feet and ending with boy on outside.
13–16	Repeat measures 9–12, reversing the directions so that boys are again on the inside.

COME LET US BE JOYFUL

Moderately

COME LET US BE JOYFUL (German)

Type: Three-person dance. Centuries-old dance; expresses ancient customs. Teaches graceful movements to music. Excellent rhythm for marching.

Source and music: (a) Van Hagen, pp. 694–695. (b) Records: RCA Victor 20448; RCA Victor LPM-1622; Folkraft 1195; Educational Dance Recordings FD-1. Piano score: See above. (6/8 time.)

Formation: Groups of three facing three, a boy between two girls.

Basic steps: Walk, skip.

Measures:

1–2   Starting on their left feet, the two groups of three dancers advance toward each other in three steps; boys bow and girls curtsy to opposites.

3–4 Two groups retire, repeating same movements.

5–8 Repeat measures 1–4.

9–12 Boy hooks right elbow with girl on right and turns her with two skip steps. Then he hooks left elbow with girl on left and turns her with two skips.

13–16 Repeat measures 9–12.

1–8 Repeat measures 1–8 but, on this advance, group drops hands, passes left shoulders with the advancing three, and continues forward to face a new group of three.

Repeat entire dance.

LA COSTILLA (Mexican)

Type: Couple line dance. Simplified form of the Mexican hat dance.

Source: As performed at the U.S.C. Dance Workshop, 1959; developed from Windsor Records description.

Music: Record: Windsor 752. (2/4 time.)

Formation: Boys in one line facing girls in another line about eight feet apart. Hats on floor directly in front of each person.

Basic steps: Walk, skip.

Measures:

PART I

1–2 All walk three steps (right, left, right) diagonally to right of hat and finish with quick dip on right foot. Then walk three steps (left, right, left) back to original position and dip on left foot.

3–4 Repeat same movements, walking straight ahead (toward own hat) and returning to original position.

5–6 Repeat again, walking left and returning.

7–8 Skip eight steps clockwise around own hat.

1 Interlude; stand still.

PART II

1–6 Repeat measures 1–6 of Part I.

7–8 Skip eight steps to partner's position. Keep to own right side of hats.

1 Interlude; stand still.

PART III

1–6 Repeat measures 1–6 of Part I.

7–8 Skip eight steps back to original position, keeping right of own hat.

1 Interlude; stand still.

PART IV

1–6 Repeat measures 1–6 of Part I.

7–8 Skip between hats to partner's position; girl picks up hat.

1 Girl puts hat on and curtsies.

TERSCHELLING REEL NO. 2 (Dutch)

Type: Couple round dance ("Swart").
Source: As performed at the U.S.C. Dance Workshop, 1958.
Music: Record: Columbia DB-1798. (2/4 time.)
Formation: Two couples in circle, holding hands, girls on boys' right.
Basic steps: Step-hop, jump, schottische, figure eight.
Measures:

1–4   Beginning on right feet, all take four step-hops counterclockwise. Swing hands up and together on count 8.

5–8   Take four step-hops clockwise. Boys end up facing one another, girls behind their partners. (G B B G)

9–14   Boys join right hands and dance alone with six step-hops. Starting with right foot, swing left foot across in front.

15–16   Boys jump three times, bringing feet together, apart, and together. On count 4, drop hands and face partner. (G B B G)

17–24   Partners perform the actions of measures 9–16.

1–4   *Figure Eight.* Take four schottische steps (step, step, step, hop), passing right shoulders and then left, and end by leaving girls in center facing one another, boys behind partners. (B G G B)

5–12   Girls repeat boys' action of measures 9–16.

13–20   Repeat action of measures 17–24, ending in a circle.

Repeat entire dance.

CALIFORNIA SCHOTTISCHE (American)

Type: Schottische. Sometimes known as the "Military Schottische." Teaches basic toe-heel movements.
Source: As performed at the U.S.C. Dance Workshop, 1955.
Music: Any good schottische record. (4/4 time.)
Formation: Varsouvienne position (see Glossary).
Basic steps: Toe-heel, walk.
Measures:

1   Point left toe forward, then out to side.

2   Boy crosses behind partner in three steps (left, right, left); hold.

3   Point right toe forward and to side.

4   Cross back (right, left, right); hold.

5–8   Repeat measures 1–4.

9–10   Walk forward and turn half around clockwise in three steps (left, right, left).

11–12   Back up counterclockwise in two steps (right, left) and turn counterclockwise (right, left, right).

13–16   Repeat measures 9–12.

Repeat from beginning.

KEN YOVDU (Israeli)

Type: Round dance.
Source: As performed at the U.S.C. Dance Workshop, 1957.
Music: Record: Israel 118A. (4/4 time.)
Formation: Single circle, hands joined.
Basic steps: Side step, hop, jump.
Measures:

Count
1   1: Step with right foot to right side.
    2: Close left foot to right; bend both knees.
    3: Step with right foot to right.
    4: Hold.
Count
2   1: Stamp left foot across in front of right, turning body slightly to right.
    2: Hop back on right foot.
    3: Hop again on right foot; bring left foot beside right.
    4: Hold.
3   Repeat measure 1.
Count
4   1: Jump with both feet, turning slightly left.
    2: Hop back on right foot; swing left forward.
    3: Hop on right; bring left alongside right.
    4: Hold.

Repeat from beginning.

LA RASPA (Mexican)

Type: Novelty couple dance.
Source: As performed at the U.S.C. Dance Workshop, 1955.
Music: Records: Methodist 106; Folkraft 1119; RCA Victor 1623; Educational Dance Recordings FD-1. (6/8 time.)
Formation: Double circle, partners facing each other, arms extended, both hands joined.
Basic steps: Jump, elbow swing.
Measures:

PART I

1   Jump with left heel forward and right foot back at the same time.
2   Jump with right heel forward and left foot back.
3–4   Jump three times, using foot changes as described in measures 1–2.
5–6   Repeat measures 1–2.
7–8   Repeat measures 3–4.
9–16   Repeat measures 1–8.

1–8 *Right-elbow swing:* step left-right-left and then right-left-right. Continue reversing footwork for eight measures.

9–16 *Left-elbow swing:* repeat measures 1–8 of Part II with left elbows
hooked.

COTTON-EYED JOE (American)

Type: Couple round dance. Popular during Civil War times. Teaches heel-
toe polka and push steps.
Source: Traditional.
Music: Records: Folkraft 1035; Imperial 1045B; Educational Dance Recordings FD-3. (2/4 time.)
Formation: Couples in close dance position. (Boys' steps are described; girls
do counterstep.)
Basic steps: Heel-toe, push step, turning polka.
Measures:
1–2 Touch left heel out to side; then touch left toe to right heel. Con-
clude with one polka step to left.
3–4 Repeat the same movements, starting with the right foot.
5–8 Turn around to the left (counterclockwise) in an individual circle,
doing four polka steps.
9–12 Take four push steps (see Glossary), moving left counterclockwise.
Take four push steps to right, clockwise.
13–16 Do four turning polkas in shoulder-waist position (turn clockwise,
advance counterclockwise).

Repeat from beginning.

PATTY CAKE POLKA (American)

Type: Play-party dance and mixer.
Source: Traditional.
Music: Record: Folkraft F1177A. (2/4 time.)
Formation: Double circle, partners facing. Both hands joined, boys' backs
to center of ring. Boys start on left feet, girls on right.
Basic step: Heel-toe.
Measures:
1–2 Heel-toe, heel-toe. (Boys use left feet, girls right.)
3–4 Slide, slide, slide, slide (counterclockwise).
5–6 Heel-toe, heel-toe. (Boys use right feet, girls left.)
7–8 Slide, slide, slide, slide (clockwise).
9 Clap right hands with partner; clap own hands.
10 Clap left hands with partner; clap own hands.
11 Clap both hands with partner; clap own hands.

12   Slap own knees.

13–14 Do right-elbow swing with partner in four steps.

15–16 Progress left to new partner in four walking steps.

Repeat from beginning.

Double circle, partners facing.

BADGER GAVOTTE (American)

Type: Early American round dance. Teaches walking steps and turning two-steps.

Reference: Van Hagen.

Music: Record: Victor 36403. (4/4 time.)

Formation: Double circle, all facing counterclockwise with boys on inside. Inside hands joined.

Basic step: Walk.

Measures:

1–2   Starting on outside foot, walk four steps counterclockwise; end facing partner on fourth step.

3–4   Slide four steps counterclockwise; end facing clockwise.

5–8   Repeat measures 1–4 moving clockwise; end facing partner.

9–16 In shoulder-waist position, do eight clockwise turning two-steps, advancing counterclockwise.

Repeat from beginning.

CSHEBOGAR (Hungarian)

Type: Round dance.
Reference: Van Hagen.
Music: Records: RCA Victor 45-6182; RCA LPM-1624; Folkraft 1196. (2/4 time.)
Formation: Single circle, all facing center; girls on boys' right, all hands joined.
Basic steps: Slide, skip, Hungarian turn.
Measures:

PART I

1–3 Starting on left foot, take six slide steps left.
4 Jump, ending with feet together.
5–7 Take six slide steps right.
8 Jump, ending with feet together.
9–10 Take four skips toward center of circle.
11–12 Take four skips back to original position.
13–16 Do Hungarian turn (see Glossary). End with partners facing in a single circle (boys facing counterclockwise, girls clockwise). Hands joined and extended.

PART II

1–4 Starting on boys' left feet and girls' right, take four draw steps toward center of circle.
5–8 Take four draw steps out.
9–10 Take two draw steps toward center.
11–12 Take two draw steps out.
13–16 Do Hungarian turn; finish with a yell.
Repeat from beginning.

FYRTUR (Norwegian)

Type: Couple dance.
Source: As presented at the U.S.C. Dance Workshop, 1956.
Music: Record: Recorded Sound Ltd. RSL-912. (3/4 time.)
Formation: Sets of two couples. Girl on right side of partner, holding hands shoulder high. All begin on left foot.
Basic steps: Draw step, chain, shoulder-waist waltz.
Measures:

PART I

1–7 Moving left, take seven draw steps.
8 Bow to opposite.
9–16 Repeat measures 1–8 to right.

PART II

1–8 *Chain.* Face partner; give right hand to partner and continue around the circle of four people, giving left hand to opposite, right to partner, left to opposite, right to partner. Execute gracefully, holding hands shoulder high.

9–12 Partners face each other and give deep, sustained bow.

13–16 *Shoulder-waist waltz.* Waltz around in a small circle, re-forming for beginning of dance on last beat.

Repeat from beginning.

HAAKE TOONE (Dutch)

Type: Couple dance.
Source: As performed at the U.S.C. Dance Workshop, 1958.
Music: Record: Recorded Sound Ltd. RSL-912 (2/4 time.)
Formation: Couples face counterclockwise, holding inside hands. Boy's free hand in pocket, girl's under apron.
Basic step: Heel-toe polka.
Measures:

1   Do heel-toe with outside foot (boy's left foot, girl's right). (1) Touch heel in front; (2) touch toe by instep; (3) step-close step-hop.

2   Do heel-toe with inside foot.

Double circle facing counterclockwise.

3–4 Repeat measures 1–2.

5–6 Girl turns clockwise in a small circle with four polka steps. She is showing off; boy watches and claps his hands.

7–8 Boy turns counterclockwise with four polka steps while girl watches admiringly and claps. Couples end facing one another.

9 Do heel-toe polka away from opposite couple (going to left).

10 Do heel-toe polka together (going to right).

11–12 Repeat measures 9–10. End in shoulder-waist position.

13–16 Do four polka steps, turning clockwise and advancing around the circle counterclockwise.

TETON MOUNTAIN STOMP (American)

Type: Progressive round dance.

Source: Originated by Doc Alumbaugh. As performed at the U.S.C. Dance Workshop, 1959.

Music: Records: Windsor A753, 7615. (4/4 time.)

Formation: Single circle, partners facing (social dance position). Boy faces counterclockwise in line of direction.

Basic steps: Walk, side-car and banjo positions.

Measures:

1–4 *In, close, in, stomp; out, close, out, stomp:* take side steps toward center of circle and back out. Boy steps with left toward center of circle, closes with right, steps with left again, stomps right next to left. He then repeats these steps, beginning on right foot and closing with left. Girl does counterstep.

5–8 *In, stomp, out, stomp:* Boy steps with left, stomps right, steps with right, stomps left. Girl does counterstep. *Walk two three four:* girl backs up in line of direction; boy follows in four walking steps.

9–12 *Banjo two three four:* with right hips adjacent, couple continues to walk forward four steps in this position, then switches to *side-car two three four:* boy stays on inside of circle but turns half-way around, walking backward in line of direction. Couple's left hips are now together; girl is walking forward, boy backward.

13–14 *Banjo two three four:* boy and girl both turn so that girl is backing up while boy is walking forward. Their right hips are now adjacent.

15–16 *Turn two three four:* boy releases girl's right hand; she turns clockwise out and drops back to boy behind. Boy goes forward to next girl.

Repeat from beginning.

PUT YOUR LITTLE FOOT (American)

Type: Couple round dance. An American version of the Varsouvienne.

Source: Traditional.

Music: Records: Folk Dancer MH-3016; Windsor 7615B; Folkraft 1165. (2/4 time.)

Formation: Varsouvienne position; boy is slightly behind and to the left side of girl, holding left hand in left, right hand in right, shoulder high.

Basic steps: Two-step, walk.

Measures:

1	Swing left foot forward and step; close with right (moving counterclockwise).
2	Swing left foot forward and step; close with right again.
3–4	Swing left foot forward and step left, right, and left. Turn RLOD, change hands, and point right foot forward.
5–8	Repeat measures 1–4, starting on right foot and moving clockwise.
9–16	Repeat measures 1–8.
17–18	Walk counterclockwise left, right, left; turn and point right.
19–20	Walk clockwise left, right, left; turn and point right.

Repeat from beginning.

HIGHLAND SCHOTTISCHE (Scottish)

Type: Schottische couple dance. A very popular dance in the United States for many years.

Reference: La Salle.

Music: Record: RCA Victor 45-6179. (4/4 time.)

Formation: Double circle of couples side by side, in ballroom position, facing counterclockwise.

Basic steps: Step-hop, schottische, shoulder-waist turn (see Glossary).

Measures:

1(a)	Hop on inside foot (boy's right foot, girl's left). Point outside toe forward and to the side.
(b)	Hop again on inside foot. Bring outside toe behind other ankle.
(c)	Hop again on inside foot, again pointing outside toe forward.
(d)	Hop once more on inside foot, bringing outside toe in front of other ankle.
2	Schottische forward (counterclockwise) starting on outside foot. At end of schottische step, turn and face opposite direction.
3–4	Repeat measures 1–2, beginning again on inside foot. Begin schottische again on outside foot. Move clockwise.
5–8	Repeat measures 1–4.
9–16	Do eight measures of step-hop turns facing counterclockwise in shoulder-waist position. Turn clockwise.

KENTWOOD SCHOTTISCHE (American)

Type: Schottische couple dance. Teaches basic schottische step.

Source: Developed by the Westchester Lariats.

Music: Any good schottische record. (4/4 time.)

Formation: Double circle facing counterclockwise, boys on inside, couples holding inside hands. Boy's part is described; girl does counterstep.

Basic step: Schottische.

Measures:

1–4 Starting on outside foot (boy's left, girl's right), take four schottische steps counterclockwise.
5 Take one schottische step away from partner.
6 Take one schottische step back to partner.
7–8 Hook right elbows and turn with partner, doing four step-hops.
9–12 Repeat measures 5–8, hooking left elbows.
13–16 Repeat measures 5–6. Turn partner and take four step-hops in banjo position.

Repeat from beginning.

KALVELIS (Lithuanian)

Type: Polka round dance. Title means "The Blacksmith." Teaches basic polka step.
Source: Los Angeles City Schools Institute Outline, 1959.
Music: Records: Folk Dancer MH-1016B; Educational Dance Recordings FD-3. (2/4 time.)
Formation: Single circle, hands joined, girl on right side of partner.
Basic step: Polka (one polka step to each measure of music; see Glossary for polka instructions).
Measures:

PART I

1–7 Do seven polkas circling counterclockwise. (Everyone begins on right foot.)
8 Stamp three times (left, right, left).
9–16 Repeat measures 1–8, circling clockwise.

PART II

1 Clap on partner's hands (left on right, then right on left).
2 Repeat measure 1 of Part II.
3–4 Hook right elbows and turn with partner, doing four skip steps.
5–8 Repeat measures 1–4 of Part II.

PART III

1–4 Boy stands in place and claps his hands. Girl does three polkas forward and then stamps three times.
5–8 Girl returns to place, doing three polkas and ending with three stamps.
9–16 Boy performs measures 1–8 of Part III while girl claps.

PART IV

1–8 Repeat Part II.

PART V

1–8 Do grand right and left for eight polkas.
9–16 Do shoulder-waist turning polka with girl met on eighth polka of Part V.

Repeat from beginning.

SOLDIER'S JOY (Virginia Reel)

Moderately Fast

VIRGINIA REEL (American)

Type: Reel. Ancestor of the square dance. Popular during colonial days.

Source: Traditional.

Music: Record: MacGregor 735A or any good square dance record. (4/4 or 2/4 time.) Piano score: See page 75.

Formation: File formation (boys in one line, girls in another, facing). Four to five couples in a set.

Basic step: Walk.

Measures: Note: Directions given for head girl and foot boy. The head boy and foot girl duplicate each movement indicated.

| Head girl | G G G G | Foot girl |
| Head boy | B B B B | Foot boy |

1–8   All walk forward four steps and then backward to original position. Repeat same movement.

1–8   Head girl and foot boy walk to center, bow, and return (walking backward) to place. (Each movement is repeated by head boy and foot girl.)

1–8   Couple meets in center, turns with linked right elbows, and returns to place.

1–8   Couple repeats previous eight measures, linking left elbows.

1–8   Couple meets in center, turns with clasped right hands, and returns to place.

1–8   Couple does do-si-do (see Glossary) and returns to place.

1–8   Head boy and girl join hands, slide (see Glossary) down the center to foot of line, and return to place. (Foot couple does not repeat this movement.)

1–32   *Reel:* head boy and girl hook right elbows and turn one and a half times. Boy then goes to girl's line, girl to boy's line. Each hooks left elbows with first person in opposite line, turns, and returns to partner for a right-elbow turn. Reel continues until head couple reaches foot of set. Then head couple joins hands and slides back to head position.

1–8   All go forward and back twice.

1–8   *March:* head boy and girl each turn toward outside and march to foot of set; others follow. Head couple joins hands and makes an arch at the foot; others march under arch. Set re-forms with original head couple at foot of set.

Dance continues until everyone has been the head couple at least once.

Virginia Reel
formation.

OH SUSANNA (American)

Type: Round dance mixer. Useful as a pre-
requisite to square dance instruction.
Reference: Folkraft records outline.
Music: Records: Folkraft 1186; RCA Victor
LPM-1623; Educational Dance Recordings SG-2. (4/4 time.)
Formation: Single circle of couples facing center, girl on partner's right side.
Basic steps: Walk, do-si-do, grand right and left.
Measures:
  1–4   Girl takes four walking steps toward center of circle, beginning on
         left foot, and then returns to place.
  5–8   Boy repeats girl's steps of measures 1–4.
  9–12 Partners do-si-do (pass right shoulders, walk around partner in eight
         steps).
13–16 Do-si-do your corners (face corner and repeat back-to-back pattern
         with corner).
17–24 Grand right and left (seven changes counting partner as first change).
25–32 Promenade with new partner.
Repeat.

Elementary Folk Dances   77

BROWN-EYED MARY (American)

Type: Round dance play-party mixer.
Source and music: Record: Folkraft 1186.*
Formation: Circle of couples, promenade position, facing counterclockwise.
   Begin on left foot.
Basic steps: Walk, promenade, corner and partner swings.
Measures:
   (Promenade throughout each verse.)

VERSE 1

1–8   "If by chance we should meet
Upon the lone prairie,
In my arms I would embrace
My darling brown-eyed Mary."

CHORUS

9–10   "Turn your partner halfway round (link right elbows),
11–12   Turn your corner lady (link left elbows);
13–14   Turn your partner all way round (link right elbows),
15–16   Promenade the forward lady (girl in front)."
Repeat.

   * Instructions used by permission of Folkraft Record Company.

Promenade in Brown-eyed Mary.

VERSE 2

1–8   "Of all the animals in the world
       I'd rather be a COON;
       I'd climb the tallest tree around
       And make eyes at the moon."

VERSE 3

1–8   "A peanut on the railroad track,
       Its heart was all a-flutter;
       Along came a choo choo train—
       Toot, toot, peanut butter."

MISIRLOU (Greek)

Type: Broken circle round dance.
Source: As performed at the U.S.C. Dance Workshop, 1955.
Music: Records: Columbia 7217; RCA Victor LPM-1620; Educational
  Dance Recordings FD-3; Elektra EKL-206. (4/4 time.)
Formation: Broken circle.
Basic steps: Walk, grapevine.
Measures:
  1   Beginning on right foot, step in place and hold. Point left toe in
      front of right foot. Move left toe in an arc back to right heel.
  2   With left foot behind right, step with right foot to the side, step with
      left in front of right, and pivot a half-turn to the left on left foot (so as
      to face clockwise).
  3–4 Take one two-step forward with right foot, moving clockwise. Take
      another two-step left (counterclockwise). End facing center.
Repeat measures 1–4 throughout dance.

GUSTAV'S SKOAL (Swedish)

Type: Square dance. Recommended for beginners. Teaches graceful move-
  ments.
Reference: Van Hagen, p. 504.
Music: Records: Victor 20988; Linden 3600-1. (2/4 time.)
Formation: Square formation. Couples are numbered 1–4 consecutively.
  Couples 1 and 3 are head couples; 2 and 4 are side couples. Begin on left
  foot.
Basic steps: Walk, arch, curtsy.
Measures:

PART I

1–2   Head couples walk toward one another in three steps (beginning on
      left feet) and curtsy.
3–4   Head couples back out three steps and curtsy.

5–8   Side couples perform measures 1–4.

9–16   Repeat measures 1–8.

1–8   Side couples raise joined inside hands, forming an arch. Head couples skip to center, take opposite girl, go under arch made by side couple (boy goes left, girl right), and then separate and return to original positions. All partners link right elbows and turn around twice.

9–16   Repeat measures 1–8 of Part II with side couple performing head couple's actions while head couple forms an arch.

Repeat the dance with side couples leading.

ACE OF DIAMONDS (Danish)

Type: Couple round dance.

Source: Traditional.

Music: Records: Victor 45-6169, 20982. (2/4 time.)

Formation: Double circle, partners facing. Boys on inside of circle, girls on outside.

Basic steps: Step-hop, face-to-face and back-to-back polka.

Measures:

1–4   Clap hands, link right elbows with partner, and turn clockwise with eight running steps.

5–8   Clap hands, link left elbows with partner, and turn counterclockwise with eight running steps.

9–12   Partners join hands and do four step-hops with boy backing up, girl going forward. (Boy starts on left foot, girl on right.)

13–16   Repeat measures 9–12 with girl backing up and boy following.

17–24   Do face-to-face, back-to-back polka (see Glossary). Some records repeat the polka for another eight measures.

Repeat from beginning.

CLAP AND TURN (Slovenian)

Type: Couple round dance.

Source: As performed by international students at U.S.C.

Music: Record: Continental C420A. (2/4 time.)

Formation: Couples in double circle, partners facing.

Basic steps: Turn, polka.

Measures:

1–2   Boy turns to his left (beginning on left foot) counterclockwise; girl turns to her right (beginning on right foot) clockwise. Turn in two steps.

3–4   Face partner, stamp three times (boy begins on left foot, girl on right).

5–6   Clap hands in back (count 1), in front (count 2), in back (count 3), in front (count 4).

7–8   Clap partner's hands three times.

9–16   Repeat measures 1–8; on measures 7–8 (15–16) clap hands together behind partner's neck.

PART II

17–32 Do shoulder-waist polka with partner.

Repeat from the beginning. The music varies; dancers must therefore be alert to counts.

Face to face and back to back.

DUBKE (Syrian)

Type: Round dance.
Source: As performed by international students at U.S.C.
Music: Record: Alkawakeb 1322B. (4/4 time.)
Formation: Broken circle. Hold hands.
Basic step: Dubke.
Measures:

1   Beginning on right foot, step sideward to the right (count 1); close left foot to right foot and at the same time turn both heels right and body left, bending the knees slightly (count 2); step with right foot to right (count 3); and stamp left foot in front of right (count 4).

2   Close left foot to right foot (count 1); hop on left foot and swing right foot to left (count 2); step with right foot to right (count 3); and close left foot to right foot (count 4).

Repeat measures 1–2 throughout dance.

Elementary Folk Dances   **81**

SPINNING WALTZ (Finnish)

Type: Couple round dance.
Source: Traditional.
Music: Records: MacGregor 607-A; Imperial 1036; World of Fun M110. (3/4 time.)
Formation: Couples facing in double circle, boy facing out. Both hands joined.
Basic step: Waltz.
Measures:

1 Boy steps left to the side and swings right foot across. Girl does counterstep.
2 Boy steps right and swings left across. (Girl steps left, swings right.)
3–4 Boy takes two draw steps left (step left, close right; step left, close right). Girl turns right (clockwise) in three steps, moving along with partner.
5–8 Repeat measures 1–4 with reverse footwork. (Boy turns while girl does draw steps in measures 7–8.)
9–10 Balance away, balance together: holding hands, step away and then together.
11–12 Banjo turn: with right hips adjacent, turn partner in six steps.
13–16 Repeat measures 9–12.
Repeat from beginning.

TEA FOR TWO (American)

Type: Progressive round dance. Used as a mixer.
Source: Traditional.
Music: Record: Windsor 7606A. (4/4 time.)
Formation: Varsouvienne position, couples facing counterclockwise, man on inside.
Basic step: Two-step.
Measures:

A. Starting with left foot, do two two-steps forward.
B. Continue in line of direction with four walking steps (beginning on left foot).
C. Continue with two two-steps.
D. On the four walking steps, boy releases girl's left hand. She turns half around clockwise, facing in while boy faces out. All join hands (with boys facing out, girls facing in).
E. All do one two-step forward, one two-step backward.
F. Hold partner's right hand but release other person's hand. Turn half around clockwise in four steps. End with boys facing in, girls facing out. All join hands again.
G. Take two-step forward, two-step backward.
H. In four walking steps, assume varsouvienne position with boy's corner girl on his left.
Repeat from beginning.

TEN PRETTY GIRLS (American)

Type: Round dance.
Source and music: Records: Folkraft 1036; MacGregor 605. (2/4 time.)
Formation: Varsouvienne position, couples facing counterclockwise in a circle.
Basic steps: Walk, brush.
Measures:

1	Tap left toe twice.
2	Cross behind partner (left, right, left).
3	Tap right toe twice.
4	Cross back to original position (right, left, right).
5–6	Take four walking steps forward (left, right, left, right).
7	Brush left foot forward.
	Brush left foot backward.
8	Stamp three times (left, right, left).

Repeat dance starting with right foot.

GARÇON VOLAGE (French)

Type: Quadrille. Title means "The Flying Lad."
Source and music: Record: Folkraft F1105.* Dance descriptions by Olga Kulbitsky. (4/4 time.)
Formation: Square of four couples, numbered 1–4 consecutively. Girl is to partner's right; at start, partners are facing.
Basic steps: Walk, cross-skip step, grand right and left.
Measures:

PART I

1–2	Do grand right and left in four walking steps, passing partner on the right and next person on the left; stop at person who was originally opposite.
3–4	Join both hands and turn opposite around clockwise with two steps; then stamp four times.
5–8	Continue grand right and left, starting left with original opposite. Meet and turn own partner in place.

PART II

1–4	Partners clap right hands, left hands, both, and own hands. Repeat pattern.
5–8	Face corner person and repeat clapping pattern.

PART III

1–2	Do four cross-skip steps in place, starting on left foot.
3–4	Join hands and turn partner in two steps. Then pass right shoulders and take two skipping steps to right-hand girl.
5–16	Repeat measures 1–4 until partners meet.

* Instructions used by permission of Folkraft Record Company.

KOROBUSHKA (Russian)

Type: Couple round dance.

Source: Traditional. Possibly developed by Russian immigrants in the United States.

Music: Records: Kismet 106; Folk Dancer MH-1059; Imperial 1022. (2/4 time.)

Formation: Double circle, partners facing with both hands joined; boy's back is to inside of circle.

Basic steps: Schottische, balance, Hungarian break step.

Measures:

PART I

1–2 Take one schottische step away from circle (boy—left, right, left, hop; girl—right, left, right, hop).

3–4 Take one schottische step toward circle (boy—right, left, right, hop; girl—left, right, left, hop).

5–6 Repeat measures 1–2.

7–8 Jump in air and cross right foot over left; jump again and come down with both feet about twenty inches apart; jump again and land with feet together.

PART II

9–10 Drop hands, do a roll right (three-step turn to the right), and clap own hands. Boy and girl go in opposite directions.

11–12 Do a roll left to face partner again, and clap own hands.

13–14 Join right hands with partner; take one step toward partner and then back.

15–16 Holding partner's right hand, change places in four walking steps.

17–24 Repeat measures 9–16.

GAY GORDONS (Scottish)

Type: Couple round dance. Simplified from original version.

Source and music: Record: Folkraft 1162.* (4/4 time.)

Formation: Couples in varsouvienne position in a circle, facing counter-clockwise.

Basic steps: Walk, two-step.

Measures:

1–2 Starting on left foot, walk four steps forward. Change hands and turn on fourth step to face clockwise.

3–4 Take four steps clockwise (beginning on left foot), and turn to face counterclockwise again.

5–8 Repeat measures 1–4.

* Instructions used by permission of Folkraft Record Company.

9–12 Boy does four two-steps forward while girl makes two turns under their joined right hands.

13–16 Turn partner clockwise with four two-steps, advancing counterclockwise.

Repeat from beginning.

7
Intermediate
folk
Dances

The dances described in this chapter are best suited for dancers who are somewhat familiar with the basic steps described in the previous chapter—that is, for those with intermediate dance skills.

The dances in this chapter have been found to be successful for all age groups. They are easy to learn and yet challenging to those who enjoy dancing. They have been arranged here in order of difficulty.

SPINNRADL (Austrian)

Type: Couple round dance.
Source: As performed at the U.S.C. Dance Workshop, 1958.
Music: Record: Zither Melodies 1897. (3/4 time.)

Formation: Double circle of partners in varsouvienne position with hands held above head level.

Basic step: Waltz. Strong accent on first count.

Measures:

1–2   Starting on left foot, each couple takes two waltz steps forward counterclockwise. Girl passes to left side of boy as they look at each other over their shoulders.

3–4   Repeat measures 1–2 with girl passing back to right side.

5–8   Couple takes four waltz steps forward with boy slightly behind girl.

9–11 Boy dances in place while girl moves counterclockwise around him, still holding same hand position.

12   Girl spins around in three steps at boy's right side as he dances in place.

13–14 Girl turns counterclockwise with two waltz steps, forming a window as she moves in line of direction.

15–16 Girl dances backward in line of direction as boy turns once under their joined arms.

17–18 Repeat measures 13–14.

19–20 Repeat measures 15–16.

21–22 With girl facing forward, couple takes two waltz steps in line of direction with hands joined and extended forward.

23–24 In two waltz steps, girl turns clockwise to meet the boy of the couple behind; her partner goes forward to the next girl.

Repeat from beginning.

KOJA KOJA (Lithuanian)

Type: Couple dance. This is a "fun" .dance usually enjoyed by everyone.

Source: Folk Arts Bazaar, Los Angeles.

Music: Record: Folkraft 1049. (2/4 time.)

Formation: Partners facing; both hands are joined.

Basic step: Polka.

Measures:

1   Starting on right foot, each partner moves to his own right with three quick steps so that left shoulders are adjacent and right arms are stretched across chest.

2   Stamp with left foot in place twice.

3   Starting on left foot, move toward left with three quick steps so that right shoulders are adjacent.

4   Stamp with right foot in place twice.

5   Repeat measure 1.

6   Bump left hips together twice.

7   Repeat measure 3.

8   Bump right hips together twice.

9–16 Assume dance position; polka around the room freely for eight polkas.

Repeat from beginning. (The record allows for five repetitions.)

WOODEN SHOES (Lithuanian)

Type: Couple round dance.
Source: Traditional.
Music: Records: Imperial 1007A; Columbia 16082F. Piano score: Van Hagen, p. 521. (2/4 time.)
Formation: Double circle facing counterclockwise. Partners' inside hands are joined and held at shoulder height; outside hands are on hips.
Basic steps: Walk, polka.
Measures:

PART I

1–4 Beginning on outside foot, walk eight steps counterclockwise.
5–8 Turn toward partner, change hands, and walk eight steps clockwise.
9–12 Face partner, join both hands at shoulder height, and turn clockwise for eight steps in a small circle.
13–16 Repeat measures 9–12, turning counterclockwise with left hands joined.

PART II

1–2 Face partner; place hands on hips.
3–4 Stamp three times (right, left, right, hold).
5–6 Repeat measures 1–2 of Part II.
7–8 Clap three times and hold on the fourth count.
9–10 Place right elbow in palm of left hand and shake right forefinger at partner three times.
11–12 Repeat measures 9–10, reversing position of hands.
13–14 Girl swings as if to hit boy's head; he squats and she turns around counterclockwise in two steps.
15–16 Boy returns to standing position while girl stands in place.
17–32 Repeat measures 1–16 of Part II. Boy and girl reverse actions of measures 13–16.

PART III

1–16 Starting on left foot, polka counterclockwise in varsouvienne position.

WEGGIS (Swiss)

Type: Couple round dance. Originated in the United States. Incorporates numerous Swiss folk-dance steps.
Source: As performed by international students at U.S.C.
Music: Records: Imperial 1008; Folk Dancer MH-1046. Piano score: Fox, p. 67. (2/4 time.)
Formation: Couples facing counterclockwise in promenade position.
Basic steps: Walk, step-hop, schottische, polka.

Measures:

PART I

1   Extend left foot forward and touch heel to floor; then touch left toe in front of right toe.

2   Take one polka step forward.

3–4   Repeat measures 1–2, reversing foot movements.

5–8   Repeat measures 1–4. End with partners facing each other in a single circle.

CHORUS

9   With hands on hips, take one schottische step sideward away from partner (boy moves left, girl right).

10   Take one schottische step toward partner and end in shoulder-waist position.

11–12   Turn clockwise with four step-hops. (Boy begins on left foot, girl on right.)

13–16   Repeat measures 9–12.

PART II

1–2   Partners are facing (boy facing counterclockwise) in a single circle, with hands joined. Boy begins on left foot, girl on right. Do a heel-toe polka toward center of circle. Keep hands pointed downward in the direction of movement.

3–4   Facing out, repeat measures 1–2 of Part II with foot movements reversed.

5–8   Repeat measures 1–4 of Part II.

CHORUS

9–16   Repeat Chorus of Part I.

PART III

1   Facing counterclockwise in promenade position, swing left foot to left in a half arc. Swing right foot across and in front of left, and touch right toe to floor.

2   Repeat measure 1 of Part III, reversing footwork.

3–4   Take two polka steps counterclockwise.

5–8   Repeat measures 1–4 of Part III.

CHORUS

9–16   Repeat Chorus of Part I. End with boy's back to center of circle, partners facing, joined right hands held high.

PART IV

1–2   Repeat measures 1–2 of Part III.

3–4   Take two polka steps clockwise, moving into partner's position.

5–8   Repeat measures 1–4 of Part IV. End in original position, ready for chorus.

9–16 Repeat Chorus of Part I. End in a double circle facing counterclockwise with inside hands joined.

PART V

1–2 Beginning on boy's left foot, girl's right, walk three steps counterclockwise. On the third step, release hands and turn (boy turns left, girl right), join hands again, and bow or curtsy.

3–4 Repeat measures 1–2 of Part V, moving clockwise and reversing direction of turns.

5–8 Repeat measures 1–4 of Part V.

CHORUS

9–16 Repeat Chorus of Part I.

KANAFASKA (Moravian)

Type: Square dance. Title is derived from the costume worn by peasant women.
Source: Traditional.
Music: Record: Imperial 1089. Piano score: Fox, p. 34. (2/4 time.)
Formation: Four couples in square formation (numbered consecutively from 1 to 4). Partners are in waltz position, facing center.
Basic steps: Slide, polka.
Measures:

PART I

1–2 Heads cross: couples 1 and 3 exchange places with four slides. Boys pass back to back.

3–4 Sides cross: couples 2 and 4 exchange places; couples 1 and 3 turn around with four walking steps.

5–6 Heads cross back: couples 1 and 3 return to original positions while couples 2 and 4 turn around.

7–8 Sides cross back: couples 2 and 4 return to original positions while 1 and 3 turn.

CHORUS

9–16 In shoulder-waist position, all four couples polka around the square counterclockwise. When back in original positions, boys lift girls in air on last count.

PART II

1–8 First boy visits: boy of couple 1 goes to girl of couple 2, polkas around circle with her (in shoulder-waist position), and lifts her as he did his own partner.

9–16 First boy visits girl of couple 3.

17–24 First boy visits girl of couple 4.

Intermediate Folk Dances **91**

25–32 First boy returns to his own partner; all couples polka around the square as before.

1–32 Each boy in turn repeats the actions of the first boy, starting with the girl on his right, for 24 measures; then all couples polka on measures 25–32.

PART III

1–8 Repeat Part I.

9–16 Repeat the Chorus.

17–24 All couples continue the polka of the Chorus but break out of the square and polka around the room. On the last count, boys lift girls as girls give a shout to end the dance.

ALEXANDROVSKY (Russian)

Type: Couple dance. Probably named for one of the Russian czars.
Source: Los Angeles City Schools Institute Outline, 1959.
Music: Records: Kismet 129; Folk Dancer MH-1057. (3/4 time.)
Formation: Partners facing. Boy is holding girl's left hand with his right.
Basic steps: Waltz, side step, step-turn.
Measures:

PART I

1–2 Beginning on boy's left foot and girl's right, partners take a step sidewards, close with the other foot, take another step sidewards, and swing the other foot forward and around to make a half turn, ending with partners in back-to-back position.

3–4 With partners back to back, take two side steps, beginning on boy's right foot and girl's left, and moving to boy's right.

5–8 Repeat measures 1–4, beginning in back-to-back position and ending with partners facing again.

9–16 Repeat measures 1–8.

PART II

1–4 Partners are facing with boy holding girl's left hand with his right. Boy takes four side steps left while girl turns clockwise under their joined hands four times.

5–8 Repeat measures 1–4, moving in the opposite direction.

9–16 Repeat measures 1–8.

PART III

1–4 In skater's position (see Glossary), waltz forward (moving counterclockwise), make a half turn in two waltz steps, and waltz backward (still moving counterclockwise) in two more waltz steps.

5–8 Repeat measures 1–4, moving clockwise.

9–16 Repeat measures 1–8.

Costumes for Russian folk dances.

PART IV

1–4   In closed position, take a side step to boy's left, step left again and pause. Then reverse these steps to return to original position.

5–8   Take four waltz steps, turning clockwise and progressing counterclockwise.

9–16 Repeat measures 1–8.

Repeat from beginning.

LITTLE MAN IN A FIX (Danish)

Type: Two-couple dance. A progressive couple dance. When the dance is repeated, each couple must find a different couple to dance with, or the man is in a fix.

Source: Burchenal, *Folk Dances of Denmark.*

Music: Records: Folk Dancer MH-1054; Educational Dance Recordings FD-4. Piano score: See page 94. (3/4 time.)

Formation: Two couples in a line but facing in opposite directions.

Basic step: Waltz.

LITTLE MAN IN A FIX

Fast Waltz

Measures:

1–8   Two boys link left elbows and each extends right arm around partner's waist; each girl places left hand on partner's right shoulder. All take eight waltz steps, turning counterclockwise.

9–14   Continuing the waltz step, boys join left hands; girls move away; each holds partner's extended right hand.

15–16   Girls swing forward, make a half turn left under boys' joined hands, and end with both couples facing center of set.

17–32   Partners balance away and together twice (see Glossary); then, in social dance position, each couple takes four waltz steps, moving to a new couple to repeat the dance.

BLACK HAWK WALTZ (American)

Type: Round dance. A popular early American dance.
Source: Los Angeles City Schools Institute Outline.
Music: Record: Folk Dancer MH-3002. (3/4 time.)
Formation: Partners in closed position. (Boy's steps are given; girl does counterpart.)
Basic step: Waltz.
Measures:

1–4 Balance on left foot forward, balance on right foot backward. Repeat.
5–8 Take four left quarter waltz steps, turning to left completely around in four waltz steps, turning counterclockwise.
9–16 Repeat measures 1–8.
17 Do cross step (couples are facing, hands joined). Step left across right (girl does opposite footwork).
18 Step right across left.
19–20 Step left across right, bring right foot to right side, step left behind right, and point right foot to right.
21–24 Beginning with right foot across left, repeat action of measures 17–20.
25–32 Repeat measures 17–24.
Repeat from beginning.

STEIREGGER (Austrian)

Type: Couple round dance.
Source: Developed by the author from a traditional folk dance. As used by the Westchester Lariats.
Music: Records: Merry-go-round 504; Folk Dancer MH-3005. (3/4 time.)
Formation: Couples in double circle facing counterclockwise. Girl's and boy's inside right hands are joined. Boy begins on left foot, girl on right.
Basic step: Small waltz step.
Measures:

1–16 Couple takes sixteen swinging walking steps counterclockwise. Couple swings joined hands forward and backward with each alternating measure.
1–16 Couples begin waltz steps. Continuing to move counterclockwise, girl does eight clockwise turns under joined hands.
1–16 Boy and girl join outstretched right arms, with hands at each other's elbows and arms at shoulder height. Both turn clockwise.
1–16 Girl with hands behind her back makes a small circle, turning counterclockwise. Boy makes two turns around the girl, moving clockwise. Boy claps his hands on each measure and flirts with girl as he moves around.
1–16 Couple moves to right, with right hands joined. Girl turns counterclockwise under joined hands and ends so that her right elbow is away from her partner. Partner's hands are joined and pointing upwards, creating a window shaped like a triangle. They dance in a

small circle, moving counterclockwise, flirting with one another through the window.

1–16 Couples assume social dance position and, turning clockwise, progress around the room counterclockwise.

KOZACKO KOLO (Yugoslavian)

Type: Broken circle round dance.
Source: As performed by international students at U.S.C.
Music: Records: Balkan 547, 551. (2/4 time.)
Formation: Broken circle, hands joined, leader at right end. Begin on right foot.
Basic steps: Leap, polka.
Measures:

1   Low leap to right (right foot), low leap to left (left foot).
2   In place—step right, step left, step right.
3   Low leap to left (left foot), low leap to right (right foot).
4   In place—step left, step right, step left.
5–8 Repeat measures 1–4.
9–12 Starting with right foot, take four polka steps to the right.
13–16 Take four polka steps obliquely to the left (starting on right foot).
Repeat from beginning.

RUMUNJSKO KOLO (Rumanian)

Type: A chain dance that originated from the Rumanian kolos of the fourteenth century.
Source: Los Angeles City Schools Institute Outline.
Music: Records: Rhythms Productions A-108; Balkan 525. (4/4 time.) .
Formation: Broken circle, leader at right end. Hands joined, facing right, all start on right foot.
Basic steps: Step-hops, cut steps.
Measures:

1–2 Moving to the right, step right and hop right, step left and hop left.
3–4 Step right, step left in back of right, step on right to side, hop on right.
5–6 Take two step-hops backward (left-right).
7   Take two steps backward (left-right).
8   Step left in front of right and hop on left at the same time, making a quarter turn right.
9   *Cut steps:* step right across as left foot is pulled backward, and step left as right is displaced forward.
10   Step right, hop right, and swing left forward.
11–12 Repeat cut steps (measures 9–10), using opposite footwork.
13–14 Repeat measures 9–10.
15–16 Stamp left foot three times and pause on the fourth count.
17–24 Repeat measures 9–16.

SELJANCICA KOLO (Yugoslavian)

Type: Broken circle round dance. Seljancica is a students' dance which means "joy of living."
Reference: Kraus, p. 78.
Music: Records: Columbia 1150F; Standard F-12002; Folk Dancer, MH-1006; Educational Dance Recordings FD-2. (2/4 time.)
Formation: Broken circle with hands joined. Begin on right foot.
Basic steps: Hop, step.
Measures:

1–2   Step right to side, step left behind right, step right to side, and hop on right, swinging left forward.
3–4   Repeat measures 1–2 to left, reversing footwork.
5–8   Repeat measures 1–4.
9–12 Balance right, left, right, left.
13–16 Starting on right foot, take eight small running steps to right.
17–20 Starting on left foot, take eight small running steps to left.

SELLENGER'S ROUND (English)

Type: Round dance. The tune for this dance can be traced back to 1450. At that time it appears to have been a favorite for the Maypole Dance.
Source: Folkraft Records outline.*
Music: Records: Folkraft 1174B; Victor LPM-1621; Educational Dance Recordings FD-3. Piano score: La Salle, p. 100. (6/8 time.)
Formation: Single circle of eight couples, girl on partner's right-hand side. All join hands, facing center of circle, with weight on right foot.
Basic steps: Run, slide, turn.
Measures:

PART I

1–4   Circle left with eight slide steps.
5–8   Circle right with eight slide steps.

CHORUS

1–2   *Balance two.* Two steps toward center (right and left).
3–4   *Back four.* Run four steps backward (called "fall back a double"). Right, left, right, left. End up facing partner.
5–6   *Balance right and left.* (Steps 1-2-3-right in place, 1-2-3-left in place. Slightly turn in right and left direction while doing steps.)
7–8   *Turn single.* Turn around clockwise with four running steps.
1–8   *Repeat chorus.*

PART II

1–4   *Forward and back.* Run four steps forward and four steps back. Start on right foot.
5–8   Repeat measures 1–4.
1–16 *Repeat chorus.*

* Instructions used by permission of Folkraft Record Company.

1–4   *Side*. Partners run four steps, passing left shoulders, and change places. In four steps return to place, passing right shoulders.
5–8   Repeat measures 1–4.
1–16 *Repeat chorus.*

1–4   *Arm right*. Hook right elbow with partner. Turn completely around using eight running steps.
5–8   *Arm left*. Hook left elbows. Turn around in eight running steps.
1–16 *Repeat chorus.*

1–4   *Circle left*. Circle left with eight slide steps.
5–8   *Circle right*. Circle right eight slide steps.
1–16 Repeat chorus. End with curtsy to partner.

GATHERING PEASCODS (English)

Type: Very Old English dance dating back to the court of King James I.
Source: Traditional.
Music: Record: Rhythms Productions A-106; RCA Victor LPM-1621. Piano score: Fox, p. 16. (4/4 time.)
Formation: Single circle. Girl on boy's right, hands joined.
Basic steps: Slide, walk.
Measures:

1–4   Slide eight steps to the left.
5–6   Turn single. Drop hands and turn around clockwise in four steps.
7–10 Join hands and slide eight steps to the right.
11–12 Repeat measures 5–6.

13–18 Boys join hands, forming an inside circle, and slide twelve steps back to their places.
19–24 Girls perform measures 13–18.
25–26 Boys walk to center (right, left, right, left). Clap hands over head on third step.
27–28 Boys walk out four steps and clap. At the same time, girls walk in four steps and clap on third count.
29–30 Girls walk out four steps and clap. At the same time, boys walk in four steps.
31–32 Girls remain in place. Boys turn clockwise with four steps ending up in starting position alongside their partners.
25–32 Repeat measures 25–32 with the girls leading the movements.

1–4   Slide. Change places within four steps, passing left shoulders. Face partner; return to original position passing right shoulders.

5–6   Turn single.

7–12 Repeat measures 1–6.

       Repeat Chorus measures 13–32 with the girls leading the movements.

PART III

(Single circle, partners facing)

1–4   Partners join right elbows, make one turn clockwise in eight running steps.

11–12 Turn single.

       Repeat chorus measures 13–32, boys leading the movements.

Grand right and left in The Hatter.

THE HATTER (Danish)

Type: Popular Danish quadrille.

Source: Traditional. Described as performed by the Westchester Lariats.

Music: Records: Rhythms Productions A-107; Folkraft 1160. Piano score: La Salle, p. 132. (2/4 time.)

Formation: Square.

Basic steps: Buzz, walk.

Measures:

PART I

1–8   All join hands and circle left in six push steps ending with a stamp left, stamp right, stamp left. (See Glossary for description of push step.)

9–16 Circle right with six push steps and three stamps (right, left, right).

CHORUS

1–2 Facing partner, stamp feet three times (left, right, left).
3–4 Clap hands six times.
5–8 Repeat measures 1–4.
9–16 Repeat measures 1–8, facing corners.
17–24 *Grand right and left.* Boy bows to partner when he meets her on the back side of square, then keeps going till he gets home.

PART II

1–8 Boy swings with partner, right hips adjacent, doing schottische steps, turning clockwise.
9–16 Boy does side-car swing with partner, left hips adjacent, turning counterclockwise.
Repeat Chorus.

PART III

1–16 *Girls' basket:* Girls form a circle in the center of the set, arms around neighbors' waists. Circle clockwise using buzz steps.
Repeat Chorus.

PART IV

1–16 *Boys' basket:* Same as Part III except men form the basket.
Repeat Chorus.

PART V

Repeat Part I, then bow to partner.

THE BLACK NAG (English)

Type: Couple dance. This is one of the most popular English country dances.
Source: As performed by international students at U.S.C.
Music: Record: Folkraft 1174. (2/4 time.)
Formation: Longways set of three couples facing the music. Couples numbered 1, 2, 3. Girl on boy's right.
Basic steps: Double step, slide, siding, arming, turn single.
Measures:

PART I

1–2 Take four running steps forward, starting on right foot.
3–4 Take four running steps backward.
5–8 Repeat measures 1–4.
9–10 Couple 1 boy faces partner, they join hands and do four sideward slides ("slips") toward music (boy's left, girl's right).
11–12 Couple 2 does four slips toward music.
13–14 Couple 3 does four slips toward music.
15–16 All drop hands; turn single.
17–24 Repeat action of measures 9–16 in reverse.

1–4 *Siding.* Partners pass left shoulders to each other's position in four running steps. In four running steps, they pass right shoulders, returning to original position.

5–8 Repeat action of measures 1–4, passing right and then left shoulders.

PART III

1–2 Boy 1 and girl 3, leading with right side, change places in four slide steps.

3–4 Boy 3 and girl 1 change places.

5–6 Couple 2 change places.

7–8 All turn single.

9–16 Repeat action of measures 1–8, returning to original positions.

PART IV

1–4 Do right-elbow swing with partner in eight running steps.

5–8 Do left-elbow swing with partner in eight running steps.

PART V

1–8 Boy 1 faces rear of line. All three boys do figure-eight reel in sixteen skipping steps. End in original position.

9–16 Girls reel same as boys in measures 1–8. Head couple goes to foot of line, ready to start the dance from beginning.

DOUBLE CLAP POLKA (Czechoslovakian)

Type: Couple dance mixer. Described as used by the author as a party mixer.

Reference: Folkraft Records outline.*

Music: Records: Folkraft F1413; Folk Dancer MH-3016; Educational Dance Recordings FD-2. (2/4 time.)

Formation: Couples scattered around the dance floor.

Basic step: Estonian polka.

Measures:

PART I

1–16 Do sixteen shoulder-waist polkas turning clockwise, advancing counterclockwise.

PART II

1–16 Do sixteen polkas counterclockwise, boy's right arm around partner's waist. Girl's left hand is on partner's right shoulder, her right hand on her right hip. Boy reaches forward with his left hand and places it on left shoulder of boy in front. Make closed circle.

PART III

1–16 Boys stop and face center of circle, clap their own hands twice. Then, extending arms sideward, each claps hand of boy on each side. Continue these claps. Girls polka clockwise around the outside circle, take new partners, and start from beginning.

* Instructions used by permission of Folkraft Record Company.

Intermediate Folk Dances   **101**

MERRY WIDOW WALTZ

Medium Tempo

MERRY WIDOW WALTZ (American)

Type: Couple dance.
Source: Traditional.
Music: Record: MacGregor 607; Columbia Album C-17; Shaw 1-101; RCA
    Victor A-317. Piano score: See above. (3/4 time.)
Formation: Couples close dance position. Boy's steps described; girl does
    countersteps.
Basic step: Waltz.
Measures:
1–4 Balance back (boy's left foot), balance forward, balance back, balance
    forward.

5–8   Open to semiclosed position, facing left. Walk left, right, left (face partner, assume social dance position), close right, left to side, close right.

9–12   Balance back on right, balance forward, balance back, balance forward.

13–16   Face reverse line of direction, semiclosed position. Walk right, left, right (assume social dance position), close left, right to side, close left.

17–20   Balance apart, together, apart, together.

21–24   Do four left quarter waltz steps.

25–32   Repeat action of measures 17–24.

Repeat from beginning.

RAKSI JAAK (Estonian)

Type: Three-person dance
Source: Descriptions obtained from international students at U.S.C.
Music: Record: Folk Dancer MH-3007. (2/4 time.)
Formation: Sets of threes, boy between two girls. All face counterclockwise, inside hands joined.
Basic steps: Estonian polka.
Measures:

CHORUS

1–8 Step on left foot, touch right to left, step on right foot, touch left to right. Walk: left, right, left, kick right forward. Walk backward: right, left, right.

PART I

1–8 Girls cross in front of boy. Girl on right arches over girl on left. Girls cross in back of boy. This time girl on left arches over girl on right. Eight polka steps complete the routine.

Repeat Chorus.

PART II

1–4 All join hands, boy moving forward, girls moving backward. All do four polkas in line of direction.
5–8 All do four polkas in reverse line of direction.

Repeat Chorus.

PART III

1–8 Girls "tuck-in," turning towards boy. All end up facing line of direction. Girls join free hands. All do four polkas forward and four polkas backward.

Repeat Chorus.

RHEINLÄNDER FOR THREE (German)

Type: Three-person dance. Originated in East Prussia.
Source: Popular version of the German Rheinländer. Described as performed by the Westchester Lariats.
Music: Record: Folk Dancer FD-12. (4/4 time.)
Formation: Sets of threes. Boy between two girls holding inside hands, facing counterclockwise.
Basic steps: Schottische, run, hop.
Measures:

PART I

A. 1–2 Beginning on the left foot, take two schottische steps diagonally to the left and then to the right.
      3–4 Take four step-hops as right-hand girl goes under arch made by

boy and left-hand girl. Left girl moves to opposite side. Boy turns under his own arm.

5–8   Repeat measures 1–4, but keep moving counterclockwise, backing up on the two schottische steps.

9–16   Repeat measures 1–8.

PART II

B. 1   Run four steps forward (L-R-L-R).

2   Boy steps in place; girls turn forward and around (in place) in four steps.

3–4   Repeat measures 1–2, but back up on the four running steps and turn in on the turns.

5–8   Repeat measures 1–4.

PART III

9–10   Do inside chain. Boy joins right hands with left-hand girl. They change places ("box-the-gnat") in two schottische steps. They bow. Outside girl turns clockwise doing step-hops.

11–12   Join left hands. Chain back.

13–14   Do outside chain. Boy joins right hands with outside girl. They do two schottische steps, change places, and bow. Inside girl turns clockwise doing step-hops.

15–16   Join left hands. Chain back.

PART IV

C. 17–24   Repeat Part I, measures 1–16.

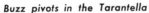

Buzz pivots in the Tarantella

D. 25   *Away.* (1) Left-hand girl goes behind boy toward outside of circle, one schottische step. (L-R-L-hop). (2) Boy goes to his left one schottische step. (3) Right-hand girl goes to her right one schottische step.

    26   *Together.* Boy and original left-hand girl do one schottische step toward each other, ending in shoulder-waist position. Right-hand girl does one schottische step across in front of other two, ending on end side of circle.

27–28   All turn clockwise in four step-hops. Girls are now on opposite sides.

29–32   Repeat action of measures 25–28.

25–32   Repeat action of measures 25–32.

NORWEGIAN MOUNTAIN MARCH (Scandinavian)

Type: Three-person dance. Movements resemble mountain climbers.

Source: Traditional.

Music: Record: RCA Victor 45-6173; RCA Victor LPM-1622; Educational Dance Recordings FD-1. (3/4 time.)

Formation: Threes, boy standing in front of two girls. Girls hold boys' hands with their outside hands. Girls' inside hands are joined. They hold hands throughout the dance.

Basic step: Waltz.

Measures:

1–8   All start on right foot; move eight waltz steps counterclockwise around the room. Boy turns his head at forty-five degree angle, each measure, toward his leading foot.

9–10   Girls form an arch; boy backs under arch; they continue waltz steps.

11–12   Girl on left moves clockwise under boy's right arm.

13–14   Girl on right turns left under boy's right arm.

15–16   Boy turns right under his own right arm, ending in original position.

17–24   Repeat action of measures 9–16.

Repeat from beginning.

OXDANSEN (Swedish)

Type: Line dance. This dance, done only by men and boys, represents a mock battle. In Sweden the freshmen in college are called oxen. Upper classmen often make them do this dance. If they smile they have to begin the dance again.

Source: Traditional.

Music: Record: Folk Dancer 1055. (2/4 time.)

Formation: Double lines, A and B, facing each other.

Basic steps: Side-steps, hops.

Measures:

PART I

1–2   A bows to B while B makes a *deep* bow to A.

3–4   Reverse the action of measures 1–2.

5–8   Repeat action of measures 1–4.

9–16   Repeat action of measures 1–8, at a faster tempo.

17–18 Fists are closed on chest, elbows are shoulder height; A takes small sideward jump to right, thrusting arms and right foot out to side. Bring left foot up to right foot, arms back to starting position.

19–20 B performs measures 17–18 in opposite direction.

21–24 Repeat action of measures 17–20.

PART II

1–2   Place hands on hips; face opposite dancer. Both jump, extending left foot forward.

3–4   Both jump, extending right foot forward.

5–8   Repeat action of measures 1–4.

9–16   Repeat action of measures 1–8, at a faster tempo.

17–24 Repeat action of Chorus.

PART III

1–2   Reach forward with right hand, taking hold of hair on head of opposite dancer. A pulls B's head forward and down.

3–4   B straightens up and at same time pulls A's head forward and down.

5–8   Repeat action of measures 1–4.

9–16   Repeat action of measures 1–8, at a faster tempo.

17–24 Repeat action of Chorus.

PART IV

1–2   Both jump, make quarter turn, touch right elbows.

3–4   Both jump, make quarter turn, touch left elbows.

5–8   Repeat action of measures 1–4.

9–16   Repeat action of measures 1–8, at a faster tempo.

17–24 Repeat action of Chorus.

PART V

1–2   A puts hands to ears; B puts one hand on top of head, the other to chin. All wiggle fingers and make faces.

3–4   A and B reverse hand positions and other action of measures 1–2.

5–8   Repeat action of measures 1–4.

9–16   Repeat action of measures 1–8, at a faster tempo.

17–24 Repeat action of Chorus.

PART VI

1–2   A swings right hand toward left ear of B. B slaps hands together, adding sound effects just as if slapped.

3–4   Reverse action of measures 1–2.

5–8   Repeat action of measures 1–4.

9–16   Repeat action of measures 1–8, at a faster tempo.

17–24 Repeat action of Chorus.

PART VII

1–16   Repeat action of Part VI, substituting fist, making appear to be hitting each other.

17–24 Repeat action of Chorus.

8

Advanced

Folk

Dances

The folk dances in this chapter are believed to be among the world's best liked and most widely known. They are slightly more complicated than the dances described in the preceding chapters. People who know basic dance skills, however, should be able to learn them without much difficulty.

These dances have tremendous popular appeal. The Lariats have presented these routines throughout the United States and have always received enthusiastic applause after each of the dances.

Many students from other countries attend the University of Southern California each year. These students have pointed out that there are several versions of each dance. Often these versions differ from those presented in the United States. In most instances, however, the differences are minor and perhaps insignificant.

When dances are used for recreation, minor changes in some parts often add to their appeal. These changes should not detract from the original version. For purposes of stage presentation, the author has made changes in two of the dances, Tinickling and the Hopak.

HINEH MA TOV (Israeli)

Type: Round dance.
Source: As taught at a California Physical Education Conference in 1958.
Record: Folk Dancer MH-1091. (2/4 time.)
Formation: Single circle, hands joined.
Basic steps: Step-bend, run.
Measures:

PART I

1–2 Moving to right on right foot, take four step-bend steps.
3–4 Continue counterclockwise with eight small running steps.
1–4 Repeat measures 1–4.

PART II

5–6 Face center of circle. Stamp right foot to center (counts 1 & 2). Step back on left foot (count 3). Step right to left foot (count 4). Step forward on left foot (counts 1 & 2). Tap right foot beside left foot (counts 3 & 4).
7 Step right foot to right side, rock weight back on left foot, step right foot across left foot.
8 Step left foot to left side, rock weight back on right foot, cross left over right.
Repeat from the beginning.

FADO BLANQUITA (Portuguese)

Type: Two-couple dance. Portuguese national dance.
Source: Described as performed by the Westchester Lariats on their national tours. Originally learned at Los Angeles Folk Dance Institute.
Music: Records: Folkraft 1173; RCA Victor LPM-1620; Educational Dance Recordings FD-4. (4/4 time.)
Formation: Two couples facing each other.
Basic step: Slow two-step.
Measures:

PART I

1–4 All four enter from four directions moving toward center. Do three two-steps. Turn clockwise in place in four walking steps.
5–8 Repeat action of measures 1–4, ending in a square formation.

9–10 Step right to side, tap left heel next to right heel. Step left to side, tap right heel next to left heel. Repeat action to right and to left.

PART III

11–19 Beginning with right foot, turn in own clockwise circle using nine basic steps.

21–24 Turn to right in three steps, then stamp. Turn to left in three steps, then stamp. Turn to right in eight steps.

PART IV—BREAK OR CHORUS

(Hands over head if not otherwise specified)

25   Hop on left foot, extend right toe to right side.
Hop on left foot, point right toe in front of left foot.
Hop on left foot, point right toe to right side.
Hop on left foot, bring right toe behind left calf.

26   Hop on left foot, extend right toe and right hand to right.
Cross right foot in front, pivot half around on both feet.

27–28 Same as measures 25–26 except opposite foot and hand movements.
Hop right, extend left toe to side.
Hop right, point left toe in front.
Hop right, extend left toe to side.
Hop right, point left toe behind right.
Hop right, extend left toe and hand.
Cross left in front, pivot half around.

29–30 Hop backward on left foot, turn half around clockwise, facing out; hop on right, walk two steps forward. Point left toe and left hand forward and down.

31–32 Repeat action of measures 29–30, reverse foot work, turn counter-clockwise.

33–40 Repeat action of measures 25–32.

PART V

1–8   Move with right shoulder adjacent to partner's right shoulder. Turn clockwise while doing three basic steps. Turn counterclockwise in individual circle in three steps.
With left shoulders adjacent, repeat the above action.

PART VI

9–10 Repeat Vamp, Part II.

PART VII

11   Step-hop on right foot toward center of square, left hand over head, right hand curved in front of body. Step-hop left backward, turn half around.

12   Turn clockwise around in three steps (right, left, right). Bring right hand above head, left hand in front of body facing out.

13–14 Repeat action of measures 11–12, doing reverse footwork.

15–18 Repeat action of measures 11–14.

Advanced Folk Dances   111

19–20 Repeat action of measures 11–12. End facing center.
21   Step to side with right foot, behind with left, to side with right. Stamp left but do not take weight on left. This action returns each person to his original right. This is a basic grapevine step.
22   Return to original position. Step left to side, right behind left, left to side, stamp right.
23–24 Repeat action of measures 21–22.

PART VIII

25–40 Repeat Chorus, Part IV:

PART IX

1–4   Hook right elbows with partner, raise left hand over head, turn clockwise in three basic steps. Break, turn left in own circle in three steps.
5–8   Hook left elbows and reverse the action.

PART X

9–10   Repeat Vamp.

PART XI

11   Kick right foot to center, step on right, hop on right.
12   Step back on left, draw right to left, step back on left, draw right to touch beside left.
13   With hands above head, turn clockwise in four steps to position of dancer on the right side of square.
14–16 Reversing the footwork, repeat action of measures 11–13, ending in own position.
17–23 Doing grapevine steps, move counterclockwise around the square. Face out one time, face in the other until home position is reached.
24   Turn in four steps at home position.

PART XII

25–40 Repeat Chorus.

VIENNESE WALTZ (Austrian)

Type: Social dance.
Source: Basic routine arranged by the author. Steps described by Bob Sorani.
    A compilation and arrangement of several original Viennese Waltz steps.
Music: "Tales From the Vienna Woods."
Record: Any dance orchestra recording. (3/4 time.)
Formation: Single circle of couples facing counterclockwise. Social dance position.
Basic step: Waltz. *Basic waltz turn:* On the waltz turn, the man's lead foot should step between his partner's feet rather than to the outside. This

is necessary for the continual pivoting. The steps in the basic turn are always forward and back, never step-side-close. *The basic turn:* step forward on left, touch in front with right, pivot (half-turn), keeping weight on left. The *rahndejahn:* step back on right, swing left foot in sideward arch, while pivoting. Bring heel in to lower leg, toe pointing down, ready to step forward on left again. The lady does opposite footwork, starting back with her right foot. The steps are executed alternately by the partners—when the man rahndejahns, the woman does a basic turn and when the lady rahndejahns the man does a basic turn.

Measures:

1–2   *Balance step:* man balances forward on left foot, lady steps back on right foot; man back on right foot, lady forward on left.

3–18 *Waltz turns:* man leads counterclockwise, stepping forward on left, lady steps back on right.

19–34 *Waltz turns:* same as above, clockwise, still progressing in line of direction. Man leads forward with right, lady steps back on left.

1–2   *Two-step out:* partners are facing, man's back is to center of circle, man's right hand and lady's left hand are joined, arms are extended near shoulder height. Man leads with left foot, swings right foot forward at end of two-step. Lady swings left foot back at end of two-step.

3–4   *Two-step back:* man steps back with right foot toward center of circle. On second measure, man turns girl counterclockwise one complete turn under his left arm.

5–6   *Two-step in reverse line of direction:* man crosses over with left foot, lady leads with right.

7–8   *Two-step in line of direction:* lady turns around (inward) and leads with left foot; man crosses right foot over left and, remaining in that position, does a two-step backward.

9–12 Lady leads with right foot, takes two walking steps (one per measure) around partner, toward center of circle. Man remains in position (right foot crossed over left), and lets partner unwind him as she walks around him. They balance *(corte)*, man stepping back on left foot, lady forward on right.

1–16 *Waltz turns with leap:* man leads clockwise, right foot forward, with one basic turn, progressing in line of direction. In second measure, man leaps back with left foot, brings right foot behind left foot sharply, and pivots, ready for basic turn leading with right foot. Partners leap alternately (with left foot)—when one leaps the other does basic turn.

17–34 *Waltz turns with leap:* same as above, counterclockwise, reversing turn, still progressing in line of direction. Leap is now with right foot.

1–8 *Mexicana:* man crosses right foot in front of left and does two-step in line of direction (woman crosses left in front of right and does two-step same direction). Following two-step, with weight on inside foot, both pivot inward and do a two-step in reverse line of direction. Repeat twice.

9–16 *Grapevine:* following last Mexicana in reverse line of direction, man keeps weight on left foot and steps back with right, progressing backward in line of direction. Lady turns inward, crossing left over right, progressing forward in line of direction. Together they progress alternately forward and backward, cross right in back of left, step back left, cross right in front of left, step back left, etc. When man goes backward, lady goes forward.

17–20 *Walk:* in conversation position take four walking steps in line of direction.

21–24 *Side-step:* in social dance position, with man's back to center of circle, take four side-steps in line of direction.

25–32 *Waltz lifts:* man leads with left foot, does clockwise waltz turns, lifting lady on first, third, fifth, and seventh measures. Lady keeps right arm down and stiff (almost straight), so man can execute lift. Lady leaps as partner lifts, both turning clockwise at same time. (Lift—basic turn, lift—basic turn, etc., man turning as he lifts.) Eight waltz steps, four lifts.

33–40 *Twinkle step:* in side-car position, do two-step away from center of circle; man leads with left, lady steps back with right. Turn; do two-step toward center of circle, man leads with right, lady steps back with left. Repeat twice.

41–48 *Swing:* in social dance position, twirl clockwise in place for eight measures.

PART V

1–4 *Walk:* in conversation position, walk four steps in line of direction.

5–6 *Roll away:* man does counterclockwise turn toward center of circle away from partner, while lady does two draw steps away from partner (back right, draw left) with right arm raised above head, left arm extended downward toward left foot.

7–8 *Roll together:* man does clockwise turn toward partner, lady does counterclockwise turn toward partner (use a three-step turn).

9–12 *Walk:* in conversation position, walk four steps in line of direction.

13–14 *Cross over:* man does a two-step in place as lady crosses over in front of partner to inside of circle in three steps, leading with left foot.

15–16 *Cross back:* man does a two-step in place as lady crosses back in front of partner to original position.

17–24 *Banjo twirl:* in banjo position, man starts clockwise with left foot forward. Couple twirls for eight measures, turning in place and leaning in direction of lead foot (use regular waltz step).

25–32 *Side-car twirl:* couple reverses counterclockwise to side-car position and twirls for eight measures as in 17–24.

33-40 *Waltz lifts:* couple executes four waltz lifts, twirling clockwise, progressing in line of direction.

41-48 *Swing:* in closed position, couple twirls clockwise in place for eight measures.

49-56 *Twirl out and curtsy:* man twirls lady counterclockwise under left arm (once or twice depending on the music). They face each other, with man on inside of circle, and curtsy.

MI PECOSITA (Mexican)

Type: Couple dance.

Source: Originally learned at Los Angeles Folk Dance Institute, 1952. This dance has been presented on many of the Westchester Lariat shows throughout the United States. Directions are as described by JoAnne Hall.

Music: Record: ASP 102. (2/4 time.)

Formation: Couples in social dance position. Advance counterclockwise around the dance floor.

Basic step: Polka. Steps described are for man. Woman does counterpart.

Measures:

PART I

1-8 In social dance position, move counterclockwise around the floor, lady backing up, man advancing. Starting on left foot, do eight polkas.

9-16 Turning clockwise, advancing counterclockwise, do eight polkas.

1-16 Repeat action of measures 1-16.

PART II

1 With man's back to center of hall, in social dance position, hop on right foot, extend left heel to side.
Hop on right foot, extend left toe to side.

2 Repeat action of measure 1.

3-4 Do four slides to man's left.

5-8 Repeat action of measures 1-4, in opposite direction.

9-32 Repeat action of measures 1-8, three more times.

PART III

1-4 With lady's back toward line of direction, in social dance position, do four polkas.

5-8 Man continues four polkas forward as lady turns right under man's left arm.

9-12 Do four clockwise turning polkas, advancing counterclockwise around the room.

13-16 Repeat action of measures 5-8.

1-16 Repeat action of measures 1-16, ending in varsouvienne position.

PART IV

1-4 Man does left heel-toe, left heel-toe. He slides four times to his left.

5–8   Repeat action of measures 1–4, moving in opposite direction on right foot.

9–32 Repeat action of measures 1–8 three more times.

PART V

1   With hands down, facing partner, leap left. Close with right; step on left.

2   Step right, close left, step right.

(Each two measures move one quarter clockwise around partner. Continue to face each other.)

3–8   Continue as in measures 1–2, ending in original position.

9–32 Repeat measures 1–8 three more times.

PART VI

1–32 In social dance position, repeat action of Part IV.

Varsouvienne position for the Neapolitan Tarantella.

NEAPOLITAN TARANTELLA (Italian)

Type: Couple dance. Popular version of Tarantella.
Source: Described as performed by the Westchester Lariats.
Music: Records: Olive 1012; Harmonica H-2051A; Elektra 206.
Formation: Couples in varsouvienne position, facing counterclockwise around the room.
Basic steps: Step-hop, buzz step, basic schottische.
Measures:

PART I

A. Hop right, hop left, walk (R-L-R), hop right moving diagonally counter-clockwise.
B. Hop left, hop right, walk (L-R-L), hop left.
C. Repeat A and B.

PART II

A. Facing partner, pas de basque to right.
B. Pas de basque to left.
C. Turn clockwise in three steps (R-L-R). End with right hip toward part-ner's right hip.
D. Step right, close left, step right, bump right hips, turn counterclockwise in four steps, end facing partner.
E. Starting on left foot, repeat A, B, C, and D (reverse foot movements), end bumping left hips.

PART III

A. Partners face each other about four feet apart. Pass right shoulders with partner in four step-hops on right foot. Right hand is extended; left leg and left hand are extended to the rear.
B. Turn to right in place in four steps.
C. Pass left shoulders in four step-hops on left foot. Right hand and right leg are extended to the rear.
D. Repeat A, B, and C.

PART IV

A. Partners face about three feet apart. Man turns right in place, doing step-hops, snapping his fingers, and flirting with partner.
B. Girl circles her partner, twirling and shaking a tambourine over his head.

PART V

Repeat action of Part I, substituting a goose-step.

PART VI

Repeat Part IV.

PART VII

Facing partner, do a buzz-step banjo swing with partner. Reverse to a side-car buzz swing.

Advanced Folk Dances 117

SICILIAN TARANTELLA (Italian)

Type: Two-couple dance. This dance dates back several hundred years. Some historians believe that its original purpose was to restore health.

Source: Traditional. Described as presented by the Westchester Lariats.

Music: Records: RCA Victor LPM-1621; Educational Dance Recordings FD-4. Piano score: Herman, p. 45. (6/8 time.)

Formation: Groups of four, couple behind couple, facing front, girl on right side.

Basic steps: Step-hop, heel-and-toe, buzz turns.

Measures:

PART I

1	Facing front, step on right foot, swing left foot across, hop right.
2	Step on left foot, swing right foot across, hop left.
3–4	*Four change steps:* step right, swing left across. Repeat to the left, to the right, and to the left.
5–8	Repeat action of measures 1–4.
1–8	Repeat action of measures 1–8.

PART II

9–10	Facing front, hop on left foot four times, making one complete turn clockwise.
11–12	Stamp right foot down and make one complete turn clockwise using pivot or buzz steps.
13–16	Repeat action of measures 9–12, turning to the left.
9–16	Repeat action of measures 9–16.

PART III

17–18	All turn backs to center of four and take four slides clockwise into the position of the person on right. Leading arm is curved over head.
19–20	Repeat *four change steps*.
21–24	Repeat action of measures 17–20, moving to the position of next person on right.
17–24	Repeat action of measures 17–24, ending in original position.

PART IV

1–2	Partners face, passing left shoulders in four skip steps. Both arms are curved over head.
3–4	Repeat *four change steps*.
5–6	Four skips backwards.
7–8	Repeat *four change steps*.
1–8	Repeat action measures 1–8.

PART V

9	Boy kneels on left knee, facing partner. Boy slaps right knee and raises right forefinger while girl slaps left knee and raises right forefinger.

10–12 Repeat action of measure 9 three more times, adding another finger on the raised hand each time.

13–16 Girl does eight skip steps counterclockwise around her partner.

9–16 Repeat action of measures 9–16.

PART VI

17–18 (Partners are turned back to back, arms raised.) Place right toe across left foot, step right; place left toe across right foot, step left.

19–20 Do four slides clockwise to partner's position.

21–24 Repeat action of measures 17–20, moving to next position.

17–24 Repeat action of measures 17–24, ending in original position.

PART VII

9 Facing front, hop on left, touch right heel to right side. Hop on left, touch right toe to right side. Repeat movement to the right. Left hand is raised overhead.

10 Repeat action of measure 9.

11–12 Stamp right foot down and make one complete turn clockwise using pivot or buzz steps.

13–16 Repeat action of measures 9–12, moving to the left, reversing footwork.

9–16 Repeat action of measures 9–16.

PART VIII

17–20 With partners facing, repeat action of measures 9–12, Part II.

21–24 Repeat action of measures 13–16, Part II.

25–32 Repeat action of measures 17–24.

TINICKLING (Philippine)

Type: Traditional two-couple dance. Originally the dance was imitative of the movements of tikling birds as they walked among tree branches.

Source: Learned from Philippine students attending U.S.C. Described as performed by the Westchester Lariats.

Music: Record: RCA Victor LPM-1619. Piano score: Tolentino, p. 350. (3/4 time.)

Equipment needed: Two eight-foot bamboo poles and two crossbars (see photograph).

Formation: A boy kneels at one end of the poles, a girl at the other. They hit the poles together on the heavy beat of the waltz music, slide them out about fifteen inches, and hit them twice on the crossbars. They must maintain perfect rhythm. The dancers step between the poles twice while the poles are being hit against the crossbars twice. The dancers step outside the poles once while the poles are being hit together.

Foot work is described for boys. Girls do counterpart.

Basic steps: Fast waltz, hop.

Measures:

STEP I

1–4   Advance toward poles in four small waltz steps. Boy begins on left foot; arms are raised waist high to his right. When boy leads with right foot on second waltz step, arms are moved to opposite side. Boy has left side to poles, girl has right side.

5   Touch left foot to floor between poles twice; lift toe once.

6–8   Repeat action of measure 5 three more times.

STEP II

1   Boy has left side to poles, girl has right. Moving sideways, boy facing center of circle, girl facing out, step between poles on left foot (count 1), then right foot (count 2), left foot on outside (count 3), moving from one side of poles to the other.

2   Step between poles on right foot (count 1), then left foot (count 2), right foot on outside of poles at starting position (count 3).

3–16   Repeat action of measures 1–2 seven more times.

STEP III

1   Running clockwise around the poles, boy crosses over poles as in Step II, measure 1.

2   Instead of coming back across, boy moves three steps (R-L-R) toward center of circle on outside of pole 2.

3   Cross over as in measure 1 (L-R-L).

4   Return to starting position in three steps (R-L-R). Girl also moves clockwise around poles. She starts down side of pole before crossing over.

5–16   Repeat action of measures 1–4 three more times, ending in original positions.

STEP IV

1–6   Boys move clockwise on outside, girls move counterclockwise on inside of circle. They take two steps between each pair of poles, then four steps to reach next set of poles. Continue to original position.

7–12   Repeat action of measures 1–6.

13–16   Repeat action of measures 1–4 in Step II.

STEP V

1–16   Repeat action of Step II.

STEP VI

1   Partners are facing each other toward center of their own pair of poles. Boy moves to his left, girl to her right. Boy jumps between the poles twice, then spreading feet apart lands outside poles. Left foot is outside pole 2, right foot is outside pole 1 as poles are hit together on count 3.

2–8   Repeat action of measure 1 seven more times. On measure 8, turn half around while in the air, ending with back toward partner's back.

9–16   Repeat action of measures 1–8. Turn half around on measure 8, ending in original position.

STEP VII

1   Boy crosses over outside pole 2, using movement of Step II, then remains on that side throughout this step. Girl steps between on right, then on left, out on right. Girl remains on outside of pole 1. They join hands.

2   Boy steps between poles (R-L), out on right. Girl steps between poles (L-R), out on left.

3–16   Continue action of measures 1–2. Boy crosses back over on measure 16. End facing partner outside pole 1.

Performing the Tinickling.

STEP VIII

1–16   Girl moves into center of own set of poles and repeats Step II throughout this part. Boy repeats action of Step III, moving clockwise around partner. On measure 16 he stops directly behind partner facing out, the same as his partner.

STEP IX

1–16   Repeat action of Step II, both facing the same direction.

HIGHLAND FLING (Scottish)

Type: Solo dance. One of Scotland's most popular traditional dances. Originally performed to encourage participants before battle.
Source: Described as performed by the Westchester Lariats.
Music: Record: RCA Victor LPM-1621. Piano score: La Salle, p. 158. (4/4 time.)
Formation: Solo. Arm curved over head, free hand on hip.
Basic step: Hop with various foot patterns for free foot.
Measures:

PART I

1   With left arm curved over head, hop on left foot, touch right toe to side; hop on left foot, raise right foot in front of left knee.
2   Hop on left foot, touch right foot to right side; hop on left foot, raise right foot in front of left knee.
3–4   Repeat action of measures 1–2 to the left, right arm curved over head.
5–6   Repeat action of measures 1–2.
7   Leap on right foot. At same time make a half turn right, left hand curved overhead, left foot behind right knee. This is called a "break turn."
8   Hop on right foot, left foot in front of right knee. Hop on right, making half turn right as left foot is brought behind left knee.

PART II

1–8   Repeat action of measures 1–8 beginning with left foot.

PART III

1   Hop on left foot, touch right toe to right side; hop on left foot, raise right foot behind left knee.
2   Hop on left foot, raise right foot in front of left knee; leap on right foot, raise left foot behind right knee.
3–4   Repeat action of measures 1–2 to the left.
5   Repeat action of measure 1.
6   Repeat break turn.
7–8   Repeat action of measures 5–6.

PART IV

9   Hop on left foot, touch right foot to right side; hop on left foot, raise right foot behind left knee.
10   Hop on left foot, raise right foot in front of left knee; hop on left foot, raise right foot behind left knee.
11–12   Repeat action of measures 9–10 to the left.
13–14   Repeat to right with a break turn.
15–16   Repeat to left with a break turn.

PART V

1   Hop on left foot, touch right toe forward; hop on left foot, raise right foot in front of left knee.

2	Hop on right foot, touch left toe forward; hop on right foot, raise left foot in front of right knee.
3–4	Repeat action of measures 1–2 to the left.
5–6	Repeat action of measures 1–2.
7	Repeat break turn to the right.
8	Repeat break turn to the left.

PART VI

9	Hop on left foot, touch right foot to right side; hop on left foot, raise right foot behind left knee.
10	Hop on left foot, raise right foot in front of left knee; hop on left foot, extend right toe forward.
11–12	Repeat action of measures 9–10 to the left.
13–16	Repeat action of measures 9–12.

PART VII

| 1–8 | Repeat Part I. |

PART VIII

| 1–4 | Repeat measures 1–4, Part II. |
| 5–8 | Do four break turns. |

MEXICAN HAT DANCE (Mexican)

Type: Traditional couple dance. The most popular dance of Mexico. It is sometimes called Jarabe Tapatio.

Source: Described as performed by Jan Arborgast and Denny Nolan on their exhibition tours. *Additional reference:* Folk Dance Federation of California, Folk Dance Camp, 1957.

Music: Record: Folkraft 1038; Imperial 1002. (6/8 time.)

Formation: Couples facing front, girl on boy's right.

Basic step: Stamp.

Measures:

PART I

| 1–16 | *Zapateado.* (Boy holds hands behind his back, girl holds her skirt.) Stamp right foot in place (count 1). Stamp left heel in front of right toe (count 2). Stamp right foot in place (count 3). Stamp left toe beside right foot (count 4). Stamp right heel in front of left foot (count 5). Stamp left foot in place (count 6). Repeat this step fifteen times. |

PART II

| 1–16 | *Zapateado moving.* Repeat Part I. At the same time pass right shoulders with partner, ending in partner's position. Return to own position. This takes two measures. Repeat this movement seven times. |

1–8 *Zapateado zig-zag.* Repeat the zapateado step, passing partner using a zig-zag step, moving beyond partner about five feet.

9–16 Return to original position using same step.

1 *Back to back.* In back-to-back position, move sideward into partner's position, as follows: Step sideward right, left in back of right, face right—kick right, kick left leg forward. Step across right with left. Turn to right, finish facing partner.

2 Repeat this step returning to original position.

3 Buzz step counterclockwise in place in four steps.

4 Buzz step clockwise in four steps.

5–16 Repeat action of measures 1–4 three times.

1 *El Barracho.* At a slower tempo, facing front, step sideward on right. Cross left behind right. Step on right forward. Step left in place. Cross right behind left. Step on left.

2–8 Repeat this step seven times.

1–8 *Side by side.* Boy starts left, girl right. Each does four push steps away from the other. Each returns to his own position in four push steps.

1–8 Boy places hat on floor in front of him. Partners face hat. Jump on both feet. Kick inside leg over hat. Bend knee of extended leg, hopping on outside foot. Kick inside leg forward. Step on inside foot. Kick outside foot forward. Hop on inside foot. Kick inside foot forward. Repeat this movement three times.

1–8 *Dancing around the hat.* Girl does buzz steps around hat. Boy claps his hands in place.

9–16 Boy does buzz steps around hat, girl claps.

2 Girl picks up hat and puts it on her head. As she picks up hat, boy swings his left leg over her head.

1–2 *The Fiesta.* Partners, side by side, skip backward four skips, then forward four skips.

3–4 Repeat measures 1–2.

5 Facing partner, touch right toe backward, touch right toe to side, touch right heel to left toe, kick right to side.

6–11 Repeat measure 5 six times.

12 Girl turns around, takes off hat and bows.

124 *Advanced Folk Dances*

Performing the Mexican Hat Dance.

HOPAK (Russian)

Type: Two-couple dance. The national dance of the Ukrainian people.

Source: Described as performed by the Westchester Lariats.

Music: Record: ASP 189.

Formation: Double circle, facing counterclockwise, two couples to a set. Number one couple works with the couple immediately behind them. Boy's left arm is extended forward; his right hand is on partner's right hip. Girl's left hand is across her chest; her right hand is on her right hip.

Basic steps: As described in each step.

Measures:

1–6 *Introduction.* Dancers do slow step-swings.

STEP I

1–16 *Pas de basque.* Beginning to right, do pas de basque steps advancing counterclockwise around the circle.

STEP II

1–16 *Hop-touch-hop-kick-run.* Hop on right foot, touch left foot forward and in front of right foot, hop on right foot, kick left foot forward, run forward left-right-left. Continue, starting next step on left foot.

STEP III

1–16 *Russian polka.* Omitting the hop, move counterclockwise around the circle doing sixteen polka steps.

1–16 *Buzz-step turn.* In banjo position, buzz swing with partner eight measures clockwise; reverse in side-car position eight measures. (Boy's right hand is on girl's left hip; his left hand is curved overhead. Girl's right hand is on boy's left shoulder; her left hand is closed and on her left hip.)

STEP V

1–16 *Girls swing.* The two girls hold hands, lean away from each other, turn clockwise for eight measures, then turn counterclockwise for eight measures. Boys stand in place and clap their hands.

STEP VI

1–16 *Boys swing.* Boys face, join right arms at shoulder height, step right, skip-kick left, step left, skip-kick right. Move counterclockwise throughout the steps.

STEP VII

1–16 *Falling step.* In original position, fall forward on left, rock back on right, kick left, run left-right-left. Continue to the opposite side.

STEP VIII

1–16 *Buzz-step turn.* Same as Step IV.

STEP IX

1–16 *Push-away step.* Face partner. Move to right eight push steps. Move to left eight push steps, ending in front of partner. Move to left, then back to right doing push steps, ending in front of partner.

STEP X

1–16 *Heel-toe-kick.* Hop left, touch right heel; hop left, touch right toe; hop left, kick right foot diagonally forward. Repeat using opposite footwork.

STEP XI

1–16 *Boys squat-stride-stand.* Boys drop to a squat position, spring up balancing weight on heels. Girls clap hands, keep time.

STEP XII

1–16 *Girls kick around boy.* Girls step-hop on left foot, kick right; step-hop on right, kick left. They move clockwise around boys. Boys kneel, clap hands, keep time.

STEP XIII

1–16 *Boys squat-run.* In a squat position, boys kick feet out in front alternately. Girls clap hands, keep time.

STEP XIV

Tight social. In tight social dance position, turn clockwise. Balance out and curtsy on last measure.

RUSSIAN PEASANT DANCE (Russian)

Type: Double circle dance. A typical vigorous Russian country dance.
Source: Learned at Folk Dance Institute conducted at U.S.C., 1958. Described as performed by the Westchester Lariats. *Additional reference:* Folk Dance Federation of California, Folk Dance Camp, 1958.
Music: Record: National 4001. (2/4 time.)
Formation: Double circle, partners facing, boy's back to center of floor.
Basic steps: Polka, buzz, draw step, skip.
Measures:
1–16 Introduction. Dancers enter and form a double circle; boys have backs to center of circle.

PART I

1–4 Stamp right foot and clap own hands four times.
5–8 Raise arms over head and skip backward eight times.
9–12 Repeat action of measures 1–4.
13–16 Do two polka steps forward, then three stamps. Finish with girl's right arm across boy's chest, her hand on his shoulder. Boy's right arm is around girl's waist, right hips are adjacent. Free hands are raised overhead. This is known as the Hungarian position.

PART II

1–8 Turning clockwise, hop on right foot, tap left toe to the floor, hop on right foot, kick left forward. Repeat this step seven times.
9–16 Repeat action of measures 1–8 in opposite direction. Left hips are adjacent, right arms are held over head. Hop on left foot.

PART III

1 Partners are facing. Boy's right hand and girl's left hand are joined. (Boy's steps are described, girl does counterpart.) Step left foot to left, close right foot to left, step left foot to left, swing all the way through on right foot, ending with back to partner (face-to-face movement).
2 Step right foot to right, close left foot to right, step right foot to right, swing on left foot and turn facing partner (back-to-back movement).

3–8   Repeat action of measures 1–2 three times.

9–16   Boy drops to left knee, girl circles boy twice, doing eight draw steps. Stepping on the left foot, draw right.

PART IV

1–8   In Varsouvienne position, facing counterclockwise, both boy and girl starting on the right foot, take eight pas de basque steps.

9–12   Hook right elbows for eight buzz-step turns.

13–16 Hook left elbows for eight buzz-step turns.

PART V

1   All facing counterclockwise, roll to right (R-L-R), kick left foot across right foot and clap.

2   Roll to left (L-R-L), kick right foot across left foot and clap.

3–8   Repeat action of measures 1–2 three times.

9–16   Partners face, take twelve push steps clockwise, end with two steps and a stamp. Arms are stretched out sideward.

PART VI

1–2   Partners face and skip backward away from each other four skips.

3–4   Take two polka steps forward.

5–8   Do banjo buzz, Hungarian swing, and four steps.

9–16   Facing counterclockwise, all do sixteen skip steps forward.

PART VII

1–4   *Boy's solo.* Girl watches, claps hands to time of music. Boy does

Performing the Russian Peasant Dance.

Prysiadkar. Squat; leap to astride position; step on left foot; spin to left.

5–8   Repeat to the right.

9–16 Series of squat-astride movements, eight in all.

PART VIII

1   *Girl's solo.* Boy kneels and claps. Girl circles boy, doing following steps: hop left, touch right, hop left, kick right.

2   Hop right, touch left, hop right, kick left.

3–16 Repeat action of measures 1–2 seven times. All end facing center of circle, girls on inside.

PART IX

Girls form basket in center. Boys hold hands, forming circle outside girls' circle.

1–8   Girls slide to right seven times and stamp. Boys slide to left seven times and stamp.

9–16 Repeat action of measures 1–8 in opposite direction. End in double circle, partners facing, girls on outside of circle.

PART X

1–16 In shoulder-waist position, turning clockwise, advancing counterclockwise, take sixteen polka steps around circle.

PART XI

1–16 Repeat action of Part III.

PART XII

1–8   Repeat action of measures 1–8, Part V.

9–16 Repeat action of measures 1–8, Part VII. End in double circle, facing counterclockwise.

PART XIII

1–16 Holding inside hands, all run counterclockwise.

1–16 Partners turn in Hungarian position.

SCHUHPLATTLER (Bavarian)

Type: Couple dance.

Source: An arrangement of numerous schuhplattler steps by Jan Arborgast for Westchester Lariat exhibitions. The shoe-slapping movements are typical of the Bavarian mountain people.

Music: Record: Phillips (Tiroler Bauerntanz) 428 008 PE. (2/4 time.)

Formation: Couples arranged around the hall.

Basic steps: Step-hops, stamps, schuhplattler movements.

Measures:

Counts   STEP I

Boys enter single file, hands on hips, form a line across the stage, doing following steps:

Advanced Folk Dances   129

1–8	1	Stamp right foot.
	2	Step on left foot.
	3	Step on right foot.
	4	Hop on right foot.
	5	Stamp left foot.
	6	Step on right foot.
	7	Step on left foot.
	8	Hop on left foot.

Repeat sequence twice.

9–16	1	Stamp right foot.
	2	Step on left foot.
	3	Step on right foot.
	4	Hop on right foot.
	5	Step on left foot.
	6	Leap backward on right foot.
	7–8	Point left foot in front, right hand upward; hold this position while girls enter.

STEP II

Girls enter opposite side of hall, hands on hips and eyes on partners.

| 17–24 | 1–8 | Do same step as boys entered doing. |
| 17–24 | 1–8 | Do four step-hops, turning clockwise in place, right hand above head, end facing partner.· |

Repeat sequence.

STEP III

Partners are facing, do opposite footwork.

25–32	1	Step on left foot.
	2	Kick right leg up, clap own hands under leg.
	3	Stamp right foot.
	4	Clap own hands.
	5	Clap right hands with partner.
	6	Clap own hands.
	7	Clap left hands with partner.
	8	Clap own hands together.
25–32	1	Hit left thigh with left hand.
	&	Hit right thigh with right hand.
	2	Hit left thigh with left hand.
	&	Hit right thigh with right hand.
	3	Bend left leg in front of right leg and hit left heel with right hand.
	4	Stamp left foot and at the same time clap both hands with partner.
	5–8	Repeat above measures using opposite footwork.

Repeat entire step.

STEP IV

Face audience. Boy and girl use same footwork.

1–8	1	Step on left foot.
	2	Bend right leg in front, hit right heel with left hand.
	3	Hit right heel with right hand at right side of body.
	4	Bend right leg behind body, hit right heel with left hand.
	5–8	Repeat above measures using opposite footwork.

Repeat sequence three times.

STEP V

9–24   In shoulder-waist position, partners move counterclockwise around the floor, doing the following step: stamp, step, step, hop. Boy starts on left foot, girl starts on right foot.

STEP VI

Face audience. Boy and girl use same footwork.

Performing the Schuhplattler.

25–32	1	Leap onto right foot.
	2	Cross left foot in air behind right foot, hitting left heel with right hand.
	3	Leap onto left foot.
	4	Cross right foot in air behind left foot, hitting right heel with left hand.
	5–8	Repeat above measures.
25–32	1	Raise right knee, hit right thigh with right hand.
	&	Hit right thigh with left hand.
	2	Hit right thigh with right hand.
	&	Hit right thigh with left hand.
	3	Leap onto right foot.
	4	Cross left foot in air behind right foot, hitting left heel with right hand.

Advanced Folk Dances   **131**

5–8   Repeat above measures using opposite footwork.
Repeat entire step.

STEP VII

Face partner.

1–8	1	Hit own thighs with both hands.
	2	Clap own hands.
	3	Clap partner's hands.
	4	Clap own hands.
	5	Hit own thighs.
	6	Clap own hands behind back.
	7	Hit sides of legs.
	8	Clap own hands in front of body.
1–8	1	Clap right hands with partner.
	2	Clap own hands.
	3	Clap left hands with partner.
	4	Clap own hands.
	5	Hit own thighs.
	6	Clap own hands.
	7	Girl claps own hands behind boy's head; boy claps own hands behind girl's waist.
	8	Clap own hands.

Repeat entire step.

STEP VIII

Face audience. Boy and girl use same footwork.

9–24	1	Stamp right.
	2	Slap side of right leg with right hand.
	3	Hit right heel in front of body with left hand. (Counts 3, 4, and 5 are done while dancer hops on left foot.)
	4	Hit right heel at side of body with right hand.
	5	Hit right heel in back of body with left hand.
	6	Slap hands, left hand ending in air head high.
	7	Leap onto right foot.
	8	Hit left heel behind body with right hand.
		Repeat sequence using opposite footwork.

Repeat entire step three times.

STEP IX

25–32   Partners hook right elbows. Boy holds girl's right hand behind his back with his left hand. Girl holds boy's right hand behind her back with her left hand. Each couple moves clockwise in place, doing the following step: stamp, step, step, hop. Both start on left foot, leaning first toward each other, then away from each other.

STEP X

1–8   Same as Step IX, using opposite hands and moving counterclockwise.

1–16	1–13	Facing audience, boys do seven push steps to left. Girls turn clockwise in place, doing step-hops and clapping their hands above their heads.
	14	Hit right heel in front with left hand.
	15	Hit right heel at side with right hand.
	16	Hit right hand in back with left hand.

Repeat, using opposite footwork and hand movements.

STEP XII

Kneel facing audience.

17–24	1	Drop to right knee on floor.
	2	Clap own hands.
	3	Slap floor with both hands.
	4	Clap own hands.
	5	Hit left thigh with left hand
	&	Hit left thigh with right hand.
	6	Hit left thigh with left hand.
	&	Hit left thigh with right hand.
	7	Hit left thigh with left hand.
	8	Clap own hands under left knee.
	9	Hit floor with left hand.
	&	Hit floor with right hand.
	10	Hit floor with left hand.
	&	Hit floor with right hand.
	11	Raise left foot, hitting left heel with right hand.
	12	Clap hands under leg.
	13	Hit left thigh with left hand.
	&	Hit left thigh with right hand.
	14	Hit left thigh with left hand.
	&	Hit left thigh with right hand.
	15	Raise left foot, hitting left heel with right hand.
	16	Clap hands under leg.
	1	Stamp left foot.
	2–12	Same as counts 2–12 above.
	13	Step left, standing up at the same time.
	14	Clap own hands.
	15	Hit own thighs.
	16	Clap own hands. Face partner.

STEP XIII

| 25–32 | Repeat Step III. |

STEP XIV

| 1–8 | Repeat Step IV three times; then step, hop, step, hop, turning clockwise in place. Girl turns around clockwise and ends the dance by sitting on boy's right knee, free hands raised in the air. |

9
Square
Dances

American square dances have their origins in England and France. Playford's *The English Dancing Master,* first published in 1651, describes three dances in square formation. Because Playford's book was very popular (seventeen editions were printed before 1729), it was probably read by some of the colonists of the New World. The French contre-dances were among the earliest to limit the number of couples to four and to establish the basic square formation. The French influence on American square dance is shown in the continued use of such terms as promenade, balance, chassé, and allemande.

The American square dance takes its characteristics and its terminology from the diverse people who dance it. Early nineteenth-century dances were mostly contre-dances, quadrilles, and cotillions. These are still popular in the New England States. The Southern colonies developed the running sets in which the caller controls all the movements. As the pioneers moved westward, significant changes were made; the dances became faster and more complicated.

Americans invented the system of calling. Originally, the dancers were given printed directions on playing cards, fans, or other items. The directions were memorized and the dances were stereotyped. But many people could not read, and others could not afford the items on which the directions were printed. Furthermore, an increasing variety of routines made it impossible for dancers to remember the exact sequence of movements.

Thus the caller became essential to the success of American square dance. Some of the calls were the well-established French words. Other calls grew out of the circumstances of the dancers. As civilization moved westward, there were not enough women to take the ladies' places, and so men were used. They wore conspicuous patches on the seats of their pants. Calls such as "Promenade to the bar and treat your partner" were heard.

We are not sure of the exact date or place that the square-dance caller was first used. We know that it was before the 1850's, because several books that describe the caller were written about that time.

Howe's *Complete Ball-room Hand Book*, written in 1858, contains several "patter" calls. Patter is the nonsensical chatter of the caller as he waits for the dancers to complete some previously called movement. The popular singing calls made their appearance in the 1870's.

Also in the 1870's the waltz and polka routines were added to the square dance. Not until the 1880's do we find a description of the buzz-step swing. Before that time a "swing your partner" consisted of joining hands and turning the partner around once.

Attempts are being made to standardize square-dance terms and movements. Although some headway has been made, the attempts have not been entirely successful. Universal terms such as "docey-doe" or "do-ci-do" have different meanings in various sections of the United States.

Even though one may encounter regional differences in the fundamental movements of square dance, the basic foundations remain the same, and the outcomes are rewarding. Many of the attributes of life which our society is seeking may be found in the square dance. The new friendships, mental relaxation, and feelings of physical well-being make square dancing a real enjoyment. Stag lines, wallflowers, and self-consciousness are forgotten when the caller yells, "Square your sets!"

FUNDAMENTALS OF SQUARE DANCE

Like most other activities, the square dance has its own terminology. It is essential that the dancer learn the meanings of terms peculiar to his locality. Terms most frequently used in square dance are promenade, allemande, grand right and left, do-si-do, ladies chain, right and left through, and so on. These terms are defined in the Glossary.

Many of the fundamentals will be explained as they are used in the dance descriptions.

In the basic position of the square, couple one always has its back to the music when it faces the center of the set. The other couples are numbered counterclockwise around the square: couple two, couple three, and couple four.

When the caller calls "Square your sets," the four couples form a square, with the woman on the right-hand 'side of her partner. Couples one and three face each other, as do couples two and four. The man's *partner* is

Basic footwork. It is recommended that beginners use basic walk steps in learning to square dance. After the nomenclature has been mastered, the two-step, shuffle, and other steps may be added. Always walk beginners through the movements before calling the dance to music.

When basic movements are indicated but not described, refer to the Glossary for description of movements.

SQUARE DANCE TERMS

The following terms must be learned before one can satisfactorily square dance. Terms not described in this section can be found in the Glossary.

The square. Imagine a four-foot square on the floor. Now visualize four couples standing equally distributed around the square. Arrange the couples so that the woman is on her partner's right, facing the center of the circle. That is the basic position for square dancing.

Home position. The men have a home base to work from in most square dances. In some dances the women also have a home base of operation. However, in other dances the women move around from one partner to another. Couple one has its back to the music.

Honor your partner. The man faces his partner. His hands are behind his back, and he does a slight bow. The woman places her left foot behind her right foot and bends her knees in a graceful bow to her partner. Usually she flairs her skirt as she makes her curtsy.

Circle. All join hands and circle to the left or right as directed by the caller.

Swing. Place your right foot on the outside of your partner's right foot. Take a social dance banjo position. Keep your right hip adjacent to your partner's right hip. Keep your right foot in front of your left foot. Use the left foot to propel a clockwise rotation.

Promenade. Partners face counterclockwise around the square. The man's right hip is adjacent to the woman's left hip. The woman's right hand is in the man's right hand; the left hands are joined underneath. They travel once around the square or to their home position on the floor.

Double circle, partners facing.

always the woman on his right. His *corner* is the woman on his left, his *opposite* is the woman straight across from him, and his *right-hand girl* is the woman to the right of his partner.

PARTS OF A SQUARE DANCE

Usually a square dance is composed of from three to six parts. The number varies from section to section of our country.

Introduction. Most squares contain an introductory part consisting of from four to sixteen measures in which the caller uses calls such as "Honor your partner," "Honor your corner," "Allemande left," "Grand right and left," and so on.

Figure. The introduction is followed by a main figure from which the dance usually takes its name. Some square dances are composed of three or four main figures.

Trimming or middle break. This is a call inserted between the figures of the dance.

Ending. This is similar to and sometimes the same as the trimming.

The swing.

Allemande left. The man takes the corner girl's left hand in his left hand and walks counterclockwise around her, ending in home position.

Grand right and left. Men face counterclockwise around the square; women face clockwise. They touch right hands and pass right shoulders. Then they touch left hands with the next person and pass left shoulders. They continue all the way around, meeting their original partners in home position unless otherwise instructed.

Do-si-do, do-sa-do, or *dos-a-dos.* There are several ways to execute this movement. The most usual is as follows: In a circle of four (two couples), the woman is on the man's right. The men face one another throughout the movement. The two women first pass left shoulders. Each then faces and joins left hands with her partner. She circles counterclockwise around her partner, coming back around facing the opposite man. She then joins right hands with her opposite and travels clockwise around him, ending facing her own partner. She then joins left hands with her partner. He places his right hand behind her and in her right hand, which is resting on her right hip. He then turns counterclockwise once around with his partner. Sometimes *do-sa-do* or *dos-a-dos* is called at the end of a grand right and left. In this circumstance, the man moves clockwise around his partner, passing right shoulders.

Do-pas-o. This can be done with two, three, or four couples in a circle. The man faces the center of the circle throughout the movement. He takes his partner's left hand in his, pulls her across in front of him, guides her across behind him and heads her toward her home position. Then he reaches forward, joins right hands with his corner, pulls her across in front of him, guides her around him clockwise, and heads her back home. He then reaches forward, takes his partner by the left hand, moves his right hand behind her back and on her right hip, and turns her counterclockwise around.

Star by the right. Join right hands in the center and move clockwise around the circle.

Ladies chain. The women touch right hands as each moves immediately

Grand right and left.

in front of the opposite man. Each woman then joins left hands with the opposite man. He places his right hand on her right hip, turning her counterclockwise around.

Other terms either will be defined as they are used or can be found in the Glossary.

TALKING-CALL SQUARE DANCES

There are two main differences between talking-call and singing-call square dances. In the talking-call square dances, the caller does not have to be able to carry a tune; it is an asset, however, if he has that ability. Of greater importance is the fact that the caller can wait for the dancers. He can add a nonsensical pattern or just hold up the next call until the dancers have completed the previously called movement. Any square dance record can be used for the traditional talking-call square dances.

Basic positions. Reading from left to right: (1) Social dance position, (2) Banjo position, (3) Varsouvienne position, (4) Side-car position, (5) Shoulder-waist position.

INTRODUCTIONS

Nearly all talking-call square dances have an introductory call that precedes the main figure of the dance. Some of the best-known introductory calls are given here.

1

Honor your partner, ladies by your side
All join hands and circle wide
    Circle left.
Circle back and don't be late
Swing your own at your front gate

2

All join hands and circle to the left
Half-way 'round and back-track yourself
Return to starting position.
Swing your own round and round
Bounce that pretty girl off the ground

3

All join hands and circle to the South
Get a little moonshine in your mouth
Break and trail along that line
Lady in the front and the gent behind
Allemande left with your left hand
Right to your partner, right and left grand
Meet your own here's what you do
Promenade them two by two

4

Clap your hands, clap your knees
Bump-si-daisy if you please.
Bump hips with partner.
Swing your corner round and round
Swing your own when you come down

5

Honor your partners and the lady by your side
Join hands and circle wide
Break and trail along that line
The lady in the lead and the gent behind
You swing yours and I'll swing mine
All around your left-hand lady *(corner)*
See-saw your pretty little taw *(partner)*
On the corner with your left hand
Allemande left.
Your partner with the right and right and left grand
Corn in the crib, wheat in the sack
Meet your honey and turn right back
Grand right and left in reverse.
You're going wrong
Right and wrong all night long
Meet your honey and sing a little song
Turn right back, you're still going wrong
Grand right and left.
Chicken on a fence post, opossum on a trail
Meet your honey and everybody sail
Promenade one and promenade all
Promenade around and balance all

6

Honors to your partners all, honors to your corners all
Join your hands and circle left half-way around the hall
Circle left you hear me say, now go back the other way
Come back home and what do you do, you swing her and she'll swing
      you
Swing your partners one and all, promenade around the hall

7

Honor right, honor left
All join hands and circle to the left
Break and swing a promenade back

8

Do-si-do with your corners all
Do-si-do with your partners all
Left hands around your corners all
Right hands around your partners all
Balance with your corners all
Swing your corners ladies all
Promenade around the hall
Right hand to your partners, grand right and left
Meet your own and pass right by
Meet her again with a gleam in your eye. Promenade

9

Eight hands up and circle to the left
Half-way around and back-track yourself
Balance off, balance again
Swing your corner like swinging on a gate
Meet your partner and promenade eight

10

All jump up and never come down
Swing your honey around
Till the hollow of your foot makes a hole in the ground
And promenade, oh, promenade

11

All eight balance, all eight swing
A left allemande
A right-hand grand
Meet your partner
And promenade

MAIN FIGURES

Every day someone is developing a new main figure for a square dance.
The odds are very much against its becoming a lasting call. However, a few
main figures have been popular for years. The following seem to have universal appeal.

CROSS OVER

The head two gents cross over
One and three change places.
And with your opposite swing
The side two gents cross over
Two and four change places.
And do the same old thing
Salute your opposite partner
Curtsy.
Salute your own sweet Jane
Swing your corner once around
And promenade the ring
In second sequence side gents lead.
In third sequence head ladies lead.
In fourth sequence side ladies lead.

LADY 'ROUND THE LADY

Honors right and honors left
Curtsy.
All join hands and circle to the left
Break and swing and promenade back
First couple out to the couple on the right
Lady 'round the lady
Go between the couple, counterclockwise around the lady.
And the gent follow up
The lady 'round the gent
Go clockwise around the gent.
And the gent cut up
He does some kind of shuffle step.
Four hands up and here we go
'Round and around and a do-si-do
On to the next
Go to couple two, then couple three, finally couple four.
Home you go
After couple four, break.
Now everybody swing
Now allemande left with your left hand
Right hand to partner and right and left grand
Meet your partner and promenade
Repeat the figure, substituting
"second couple," "third couple," "fourth couple."

SALLY GOODIN

First gent out to the right
Swing Sally Goodin
Right back now and swing your taw
Now the girl from Arkansas *(girl on left)*
Right back now and swing your taw *(partner)*
Now go 'cross, swing grandma *(opposite girl)*
You ain't swung her since 'way last fall
Right back now and swing your taw
Dos-a-dos your left-hand girl
Right back now with a partner whirl
And promenade that pretty little thing

SWING AT THE WALL

First couple out to the couple on the right
Around that couple
> *Woman goes on outside of man, man on outside of woman.*
And swing at the wall
Through that couple
> *Swing between the couple.*
And swing in the hall
Circle four, oh, circle four
Do-si-do with the gent you know
The lady goes si and the gent goes do
And on to the next *(To couple three.)*
> *Repeat and change last line to*
> *"Balance home," after couple four has been visited.*
And everybody swing
A left allemande
And a right-hand grand
Promenade eight when you come straight
> *Repeat for couples two, three, and four.*

THE GIRL I LEFT BEHIND ME

First couple to the couple on the right
And balance there so kindly *(Bow.)*
Pass right through and balance too
> *Go between couple two.*
And swing that girl behind you
Now four hands up and here we go
Around and around and a do-si-do
And on to the next

And everybody swing
Now promenade in single file
And just let me remind you
To turn right back in the same old track
And swing that girl behind you
> *Repeat for couples two, three, and four.*

BIRDIE IN A CAGE

Up and down and around and around
Allemande left and allemande aye
Ingo, bingo, six penny high
Big pig, little pig, root hog or die
First couple a balance swing
Lead right out to the right of the ring
With a birdie in a cage
> *Girl one goes to center of circle.*

And three hands 'round
> *Man one and couple two form a circle around girl one.*

The bird hop out and the crow hop in
> *Man one goes into circle, girl goes out.*

The crow hop out and circle again
> *Man joins the circle.*

Do-si-do with the gent you know.
Ladies go si and the gents go do
On to the next
> *Repeat, using couple two as the active couple, then couple three,*
> *then couple four.*

DIVE FOR THE OYSTER

INTRODUCTION

All jump up and never come down
Now swing your honey off the ground
Allemande left with your left hand
Right to your partner, right and left grand
Meet your partner and promenade

FIGURE

First couple out to the couple on the right
Dive for the oyster
Dip for the clam
Now dive for the sardine, and take a full can

Four hand up and here we go
Round and around with a do-si-do
Now on to the next

> *After couple one has danced with couples three and four they return home; then the introduction is repeated. Couples two, three, and four take turns doing the same figure.*

ADAM AND EVE

Big foot up and the little foot down
Grab your honey go 'round and 'round
Allemande left as you come 'round
Then promenade around the town

First lady out to the couple on the right
Swing old Adam with all your might *(Right elbow.)*
With a left elbow swing Miss Eve
Now swing old Adam before you leave

Then right back home and swing your own

> *Continue around the set to the third and then the fourth couple.*

TWO GENTS SWING WITH ELBOW SWING

First couple lead out to the right
Two gents with an elbow swing *(right elbows)*
Opposite partners left elbow swing
Now the two gents with the same old thing
And now your partners everybody swing

Same two couples circle four
Do-si-do with the gents you know
Then swing your partner and home you go

> *Everybody swing, then on to the next couple.*

FIGURE EIGHT

First couple lead to the couple on the right
And circle four and don't get sore
When you come around pick up two more
Circle six and when you get straight
Around that lady and do a figure eight

> *Go between couple four, turn counterclockwise, go back between, and turn clockwise around the man.*

Around that gent and don't be late and
Back to the center and do a figure eight
Circle eight when you get straight and
Do-si-do and don't be late

TEXAS STAR

Ladies to the center and back to the bar
Gents to the center and form a star
With a right hand across and how-do-you-do
Now back with the left and how are you
Meet your honey and pass her by and
Catch that next gal on the fly
   Arm is around right-hand lady.
The gents swing out and the ladies swing in
And form that Texas star again
   Clockwise turn, ladies on inside.
The ladies swing out and right back in and
Form that Texas star again *(counterclockwise)*
Swing your partner, 'round and 'round
Promenade your partner 'round the town
   Repeat three times and you are back with original partner.

CROW IN THE CAGE

The first couple out, balance and swing
Gent leads out to the right of the ring
Swing your right-hand lady with a right-hand
         swing
Your left-hand lady with a left-hand swing
Your opposite lady with a two-hand swing
Swing your partner and put her in the ring
Crow in the cage, seven hands around
Crow hops out and the bird hops in
Seven hands up and you're gone again
Bird hops out with a left allemande
A right to your partner with a right and left
         grand
Oats in the barn, wheat in the stack
When you meet your partner turn right back
   Grand right and left in reverse.
Up the river and around the bend
Meet your partner and turn again
   Grand right and left.
Now you are right and now you are wrong
When you meet your partner
Promenade home

HALL'S SQUARE

(An exhibition square arranged by Nancy Hall)

Honor your partner and lady by your side
All join hands and circle wide
Put a shuffle in your feet as you circle south
Get a little sunshine in your mouth

Listen gang to what I say
You're going wrong, go the other way

Swing your partner 'round and 'round
Allemande left when you come 'round *(or* down)
Right to your partner, right and left grand

Meet your partner with a do-si-do
     Go around partner, passing right shoulders.
Now take her in your arms and around you go *(Swing.)*

Promenade around the floor
When you get home why swing some more

Ladies to the center and back to the bar
Gents to the center with a right-hand star

Back by the left, but not too far
Pick up your partner as you go by
And form a star on the fly

Gents back out and the ladies walk in
Form that Texas star again
Ladies back out and the gents walk in
Form that Texas star again

Heads wheel out like a rising tide
Come back in behind the sides
Sides wheel out a boy and a girl
Come back in make the waters whirl

Heads wheel out just once more
Come back in as you did before
Sides wheel out one more time
Come back in you're doing fine

One like Venus one like Mars
Head lady out and make two stars

I never saw a prettier sight
Than these stars turning through the night
Mesh those gears and make them spin

Promenade when you meet again
When you get home here's what you do
Honor your partner—corners too
Now wave to that girl across from you

Longways formation.

LARIAT SPECIAL

(An exhibition square arranged by the author for the Westchester Lariats)

Honor your partner, to your corner smile
Join hands and circle left awhile
Turn right back in a single file
Ladies in the lead Indian style

Big foot up and the little foot down
Make that big foot jar the ground
Face your taw pretty little squaw
Promenade to Arkansas

All couples balance and all couples swing
Back to back on the outside ring
Slap your hands and slap your knees
Bump-si-daisy if you please

Swing on the corner both low and high
It's a right and left as you pass 'em by
Girls throw your partners up in the sky
Do-si-do a girl and a guy

Then an allemande left alamo style
Right to your honey and balance awhile
Balance in and balance out
Turn with the right-hand half about

Balance out and balance in
Turn with the left hand half again
Allemande left pass back to your girl
Then everybody butterfly whirl

The girls whirl right, the gents whirl left
Let's call it a Lariat grand right and left

Meet your own here's what you do
It's back to back hook elbows too
With a lit and a spin out there in the blue
Spin her around that's what you do

Now gents to the center, left star around
Girls on the outside, twirl the town
Meet your partner with a do-si-do
Left star promenade, and around you go

Heads wheel out like a rising tide
Come back in behind the sides
Sides wheel out a boy and a girl
Come back in make the waters whirl

Heads wheel out just once more
Come back in as you did before
Sides wheel out just one more time
Come back in you're doing fine
Break with your left in the center of the ring
Everybody yell and swing

One and two and three and four
Cage your gals in the center of the floor
> *Girls face, holding each other's forearms. Boys, behind their
> partners, hold each other's hands. Couples turn clockwise with
> fast turns.*

Break in the center, it's an old cartwheel
    Girls do cartwheels to opposite positions.
Gents promenade right around the field
Girls line up in the center of the ring
Hang on tight, it's a Lariat swing
    Girls' hands are locked behind boys' necks, boys' hands are
    around girls' waists.

Set them down outside the ring
A whirl and a swing with the pretty little thing

Ladies star right in the center of the set
Two gents turn in a little side bet
    Man one to man two, three to four; do right elbow swing.

It's an old soft shoe that wins the girl
    Do any kind of clog or shuffle step.
Break in the center and everybody whirl

Side gents to the left of the ring
Three in a line, listen to me sing
Forward six and back you march
Gents go forward and make an arch

Side ladies chain across the ring
Gents turn, head ladies do the same
Chain them back and don't be slow
Everybody do-si-do

First and third you bow and swing
Lead right out to the right of the ring
Ladies bow and the gents duck under
Hug those gals and go like thunder

Break in the center, four in a ring
Do-pas-o with the pretty little thing
Partners left, corners right
Swing your girl but not all night

Side gents right with an elbow swing
Opposite lady same old thing
Back in the center with your arm around
Partners left, you're homeward bound

Allemande left, then heads to the right
Hook four in a line, gals take a flight

Flip the girls to a Westchester star
    Back-to-back swing, elbows hooked.
Turn them around but not too far
Girls swing out and bunch the men
Turn that star around again

Sweep the girls in hands up high
Build 'em a teepee, don't be shy
Chiefs duck under on heel and toe
Hurry up, Indian, don't be slow

In and out all around the ring
Bow to your corner and the pretty little thing

AMERICAN SQUARE

(An exhibition square arranged by the author)

Honor your partner, corners too
Sashay partners half-way through
Bow to the girl to the right of you
Re-sashay, that's what you do

Allemande left and right to your girl
It's a wagon wheel, make it whirl
You whirl 'em high, and whirl 'em low
Spin that gal in calico

Spread that star out through the night
The gals duck under and star by the right
All the way 'round to the same old guy
Roll promenade with the blue-tail fly

First and third you bow and swing
Into the middle and back to the ring
Do a right and left through across the floor
Sides divide and line up four

Forward eight and back like that
Forward again and box the gnat
Same little lady and a do-sa-do
It's back to back and around you go

Now pass through across the set
And everybody turn to the left
Fall right in single file
Left-hand star and spin it awhile

One like Venus and one like Mars
Head ladies out and make two stars
Turn those stars about
Gents lead in and the ladies out

Turn those stars about
Ladies lead in and the gents lead out
I never saw a prettier sight
Than these stars turning through the night

Partners left and corners right
Turn that gal with all your might
Now give your partner a great big swing
Then a right and left go 'round the ring
Meet your own with a do-sa-do
Take her in your arms and home you go

Side couples balance, sides swing
Lead right out to the right of the ring
Circle half and don't you blunder
Inside arch and the outside under

Inside high and the outside low
Dip and dive and away you go
Inside high and the outside low
One more change and home you go

All couples balance, all couples swing
Gents circle left the inside ring
Girls back in and take a little ride *(See illustration.)*
Put them down boys on the other side

Allemande left and a right to your taw
Bunch those gals and balance all
The Westchester stars go 'round for Hall
Ladies swing out and bunch the men
Turn that star 'round again
When you reach your place in the ring
Give that pretty little girl a swing

Basket position.

Mesh those gears and make them spin
Promenade when you meet again

First and third bow and swing
Lead right out to the right of the ring
Keep your lady on your right
Gents hook arms and hang on tight

Turn it around like a weather vane
It's cloudy in the east and looks like rain

Inside hook arms and make one line
Turn it around you're doing fine
Turn it around like a garden gate
Be sure to keep it nice and straight

Break in the center as you did before
Turn again two lines of four

Left hands high and the ladies duck under
Eight hands star without a blunder
One over here and one over yonder

Ladies change and don't go wrong
It's a right-hand star now sing a little song
Gents reach back with your left hand
It's a do-pas-o from where you stand

"Take a ride" position.

Eight hands cross, 'round you go
Grab that hand and clasp it
Ladies bow, the gents know how
You make a Lariat basket *(See illustration.)*

It's a high, it's a low
'Round and 'round you go
Shake it, make it, swing it, break it
Onward home you go

Now swing that girl up on your back
Swing her 'round like grain in a sack
Drop her down Lariat style
Spin her again for a little while

Sit her down in the ring
Bow to your corner and the pretty little thing

WESTERN SQUARE

(An exhibition square arranged by the author)

All couples balance and all couples swing
Back to back on the outside ring
Slap your hands and slap your knees
Bump-si-daisy if you please

Allemande left with your left hand
Right to your partner, right and left grand
Corn in the crib and meat in the stack
Meet your partner and turn right back

Steamboat coming around the bend
Meet your partner, turn back again
Mom's at home washing the dishes
Pop's at the river catching fishes

Ace of diamonds, jack of spades
Meet your partner and promenade
Button your shoes and pull up your socks
Swing your partner until she rocks

Now the opposite gent with an elbow swing
Go twice around with the bald-headed thing
Star right back in the center of the ring
When you get home everybody swing

All join hands and away you go
Break this up with a do-pas-o
Partners left, then corners right
Turn your partner with all your might

Promenade to your place in the ring
Twirl that girl, then everybody swing
Swing her high and swing her low
Swing that gal in calico

First and third to the right you're bound
Circle four just half-way 'round
Inside high and outside low
Join in the middle and around you go

Once around and then pass through
To a right-hand star with the outside two
Back with the left, down the same old lane
Leave that star and the ladies chain

Chain 'em over and chain 'em back
They'll snuggle and purr like a pussy cat
It's an elbow hook and make it strong
Hook on the sides and take 'em along

Hi-diddle-diddle, the cat and the fiddle
When you get home break in the middle
Circle four and you make it go
Break right into a do-si-do

Turn your own with your left hand
Opposite right, you're doing grand
Here's your partner the pretty little thing
Twirl her into a four-hand ring

Now cage those gals and away you go
Keep them on their heel and toe
The faster you go the better you feel
Break with a swing when you hear her squeal

Head girls swing Adam, then ole Eve
Swing ole Adam again if you please
Hurry on home to your partner's knees
Hug 'em, slap 'em, laugh with glee

Two and four swing that girl
'Round and 'round in your own little world
Then out to the right with a four-hand ring
Right fore arm with your own sweet thing

It's a wagon wheel and you make it spin
Gents back out and the ladies go in
A full turn 'round and you're gone again
When you get home everybody spin

Ladies chain but not too far
Come right back in a right-hand star
Gents reach back with your left hand
It's a do-pas-o from where you stand

Partners left, corners by the right
Turn your own, don't take all night
Twirl 'em to the center back to back
Gents run around the outside track

Chicken in the bread tray picking up dough
Granny does your dog bite no child no
Dance a little bit and watch her smile
Step right up and swing a while

Gents circle left, pretty little ring
Gals go right, it's the same old thing
Hurry along Grandma can't you see
You're not the girl you used to be

Rope the yearling, brand the calf
Meet your partner with a one and half
One and half and a half all around
Keep that calico off the ground

Here I come in my little red wagon
Hind wheel broke and the axle dragging
Told my Pa when I left town
Darn good wagon but about broke down

Here they come in their old jalopy
Shirttails out, now ain't they sloppy
Ace is high and the dance low
Swing that gal in calico

Ladies to the center and the gents take a walk
Take hold of hands as you hear me talk
Girls sit down and take a little ride
Move along boys, she's by your side

Twice around with the pretty little thing
Set her down when you hear me sing
Do-si-do with your pretty little girl
Swing her out then let her whirl

Two and four bow and swing
Right and left through across the ring
Break at the head here's what we do
One straight line all of you

Ladies and gents here we go
Great big kick in the middle of the floor
Kick 'em high and kick 'em low
There's one more kick to go

Thread the needle boys, sew a straight line
There's one more fancy stitch, you're doing mighty fine

Listen to me gang, here's what you do
Honor those people that's been watching you

Square Dances   157

The trimming or middle break, the movement that is called between figures, is often used as an ending to a square dance. The following breaks and endings are among the most popular.

1

Form a ring, a great big ring, and break that ring with a corner swing
Now form a ring, a great big ring, and break that ring with a corner swing
Form a ring, a great big ring, and all four boys listen to the call and swing your opposite across the hall and promenade to you know where and I don't care and find that little girl an easy chair

2

Swing your corner with your left hand
Your partner right, and a right and left grand
Hind wheels off and axle draggin'
Oh, promenade, oh, promenade home

3

Allemande left with your left hand
Right to your partner and a right and left grand
First ole Sal, then ole Sue, grab that gal with the rundown shoe and promenade right off the floor

4

All around your left-hand lady
See-saw your pretty little taw
Now on our corner with your left hand
A right to your partner and a right and left grand
Shingles on the roof, paper on the wall
Meet your partner and promenade all

5

Balance one, balance all
Swing your opposite across the hall
Now your own if she's not too small
And promenade, boys, promenade

6

And swing 'em all night
Allemande left, go left and right
Hand over hand around the ring
Hand over hand with the dear little thing
Promenade eight when you get straight

7

Now balance home and everybody swing
Now swing on the corner like swinging on the gate
And now your own if you're not too late
Allemande left with your left hand
Right hand to partner and right and left grand
Meet your honey and promenade
(Repeat 2 and 3 entirely for second, third, and fourth couples)

8

Form a ring, a pretty little ring
Break that ring with a corner swing
Ring, ring, pretty little ring
Break that ring with a corner swing
Form a ring, a pretty little ring
Break that ring with a corner swing
Ring, ring, pretty little ring
Break that ring with a corner swing
Form a ring and make it go
Break that ring with a do-pas-o
Now you're right, and now you're wrong
One more change and head for home

9

Form a star with the right hand across
Back with the left and don't get lost
Right hand back to the lady left
Break with the left and pull her through
Shuffle along the old shoo-shoo
Now you're doing the do-si-do
A little bit o' heel and little bit o' toe
One more change and home you go

10

Up the river and around the bend
All join hands and we're gone again
Break and trail single file
The lady in the lead Indian style and
Turn right back and swing 'em awhile
Promenade single file
Lady in the lead Indian style and
Form a ring, a great big ring and
Break that ring with a corner swing
Form a ring, a great big ring and
Break that ring with a corner swing

Form a ring and spread out wide
And do-si-do on all four sides
Do-si high and do-si low
With four little gents you ought to know
Chase that rabbit, chase that squirrel
Chase that pretty girl 'round the world
Now you're right and now you're wrong
One more change and travel home

SINGING-CALL SQUARE DANCES

In singing-call square dances, the caller gives the directions for the dance in rhythm with the music. The dancers must keep up with the calls because the caller cannot slow down his directions.

The dances in this chapter are described as arranged by the makers of the recordings. If problems occur in determining the movements, refer to the Glossary.

Singing-call square dances are among the most popular folk dances. New arrangements are made all the time, and old movements are adapted to new tunes. Keep up with the new dances to add interest in your dance club.

HOT TIME IN THE OLD TOWN TONIGHT

Source and music: Record: Windsor * 7415, 4415 ("Just For Dancing").

OPENER

Let's all join hands and circle to the left
Break that ring and swing, with the girl you love the best
Then you promenade back home, with the cutest gal in sight
There'll be a hot time in the old town tonight

FIGURE

Oh, the first couple right, and circle four hands 'round
Pick up two more, and circle six hands 'round
Pick up two more and circle eight hands 'round
There'll be a hot time in the old town tonight

BREAK

It's the allemande left with the lady on your left (Hey!)
Usual allemande left with corners, all shout "Hey!" on drum crash.
Allemande right with the lady on your right (Hey!)
Pass partners by right shoulders without touching, do an allemande right with right-hand lady. All shout "Hey!" on drum crash.

* Used by permission of Windsor Records, Temple City, California.

Allemande left with the lady on your left (Hey!)
> *Pass partners by left shoulders without touching, do an alle- mande left with corner. All shout "Hey!" on drum crash.*

Then a grand ol' right and left, go round the ring
> *Usual grand right and left.*

When you meet your honey, you do-sa-do around
Take her in your arms and swing her off the ground
Promenade back home, with the sweetest gal in sight
There'll be a hot time in the old town tonight
> *Repeat figure with second couple leading out. Repeat break.*
> *Repeat figure with third couple leading out. Repeat break.*
> *Repeat figure with fourth couple leading out. Repeat break.*

CLOSER

Now you all join hands, and stretch the ring w—a—y out
> *All join hands in a ring, then stretch the ring as wide out as possible.*

Rush in to the center—and everybody shout!
> *With hands still joined and raised high, all rush to center in a tight group and loudly shout "Hey!"*

Back right out and swing, with the cutest gal in sight
There's been a hot time in the old town tonight!

SAY HOWDY

Source: By Johnny Schultz, Phoenix, Arizona.
Music: Record: MacGregor * 781-B, 782-B, 7815-B, 7825-B.

INTRODUCTION

Now you bow and swing, you say "Howdy" *(waist swing)*
Your corners do-sa-do *(right shoulders back to back)*
You swing your honey around and around
The gents star left, you know *(palm star)*
You do a right and left grand—all around that ring *(starting with original partner)*

FIGURE

Head couples back to back—and then you separate
Go half-way 'round and swing *(waist swing)*
Then you trail on through to your corner girl
You swing that pretty little thing *(original corner)*
> *Passing right shoulders, the head couples cross to their home positions. Then the ladies move to the left, passing in front of their partners, and the gents move to the right, passing in back of their partners. In many areas this is the same as the "cross- trail."*

The gents star left, you go once around
Take her home with you *(star promenade)*
Balance her out that way
Swing her and she will say
"Gee, I'm glad to meet you"

>Sequence: introduction, figure twice for head couples, introduction, figure twice for side couples, introduction.

SILVER BELLS

Source: By Johnny Schultz, Phoenix, Arizona.
Music: Record: Old Timer * 8113, 8114.
Note: Once this dance starts, do not stop at home; just keep promenading until the following command is given.

INTRODUCTION, BREAK, AND ENDING

You docey 'round your corner, then form a great big ring
>*Right shoulder around corner, then join hands with partner and corner.*

Circle left go half-way 'round, then give your own a swing *(hip swing)*
And now you allemande left your corner, then promenade ole Nell
>   *(partner)*
You promenade this gal with silver bells

DANCE

And now the four little ladies star by the right
Go once around the track
>*The ladies step across in front of their partners to a right-hand star in the center; gents keep promenading.*

A left hand turn your partner—to your corner box the gnat
>*Turn your partner half around and box the gnat—with a right hand—with your corner. You will be facing in grand right and left position, in a right hand balance with your corner.*

Then do a grand old right and left until you meet this Belle
>*Pull your corner by into a grand right and left until you meet this same corner with a right hand and promenade this girl for your new partner.*

You promenade this gal instead of Nell

And now you allemande left your corner, then walk right by your
>   own
>*Pass partner right shoulder.*

You docey 'round your right-hand girl, go back hip swing your own
And now the gents star left go once around until you meet ole Nell
You promenade this gal with silver bells

>*Repeat: Dance, break, dance, dance, ending.*

* **Used by permission of Old Timer Records, Phoenix, Arizona.**

Broken circle formation.

HURRY, HURRY, HURRY

Source and music: Record: MacGregor * 657-A.

FILLER

Allemande left the corner
And a right hand to your own
Grand right and left around the ring
It's on your way you roam
And when you meet your honey boys
You do-sa-do 'round
Then you promenade that pretty lady home
   Add four-bar tag.

* Used by permission of MacGregor Records, Los Angeles, California.

Now the first old couple out to the right
And circle four hands 'round
You leave her there, go on to the next
And circle three hands 'round

> *Gent one leaves the circle of four and continues on to couple*
> *three. Couple two and lady one stand in a line of three.*

Take that couple on with you, you circle five hands 'round

> *Gent one takes couple three to couple four. They join hands and*
> *circle once around.*

Now the gent goes over to join that line of three

> *Gent one goes across the set and stands next to lady one (two*
> *lines of four).*

Oh, you chain the gals across the set but don't return

> *Touching right hands, passing right shoulders, the ladies chain*
> *across to their opposite gents. The gents turn the ladies three-*
> *fourths around and into position to chain them down the line.*

Turn and chain 'em down the line and—watch 'em churn

> *The ladies chain to the next gent in line. The gents turn the*
> *ladies three-fourths around.*

You chain the gals across the set, on your way you roam

> *The ladies chain across the set to the gents directly opposite.*
> *The gents turn the ladies three-fourths around.*

Now chain the line and swing your honey home

> *The ladies chain to their partners and swing.*

> *Repeat first part, then couples two, three, and four take their*
> *turns leading the figure.*

JESSIE POLKA SQUARE

Source and music: Record: MacGregor * 657-B.

Now the side couples arch, head couples duck right under
And you dip and you dive
Home you go and don't you blunder

> *Couples two and four make arches and move to left clockwise*
> *around square as couples one and three duck under the arches,*
> *moving to right counterclockwise. Then couples one and three*
> *make arches, and two and four duck under. Repeat until all*
> *return home.*

Now you allemande left, put your arms around your partner
In a star promenade do the Jessie Polka Dance

* Used by permission of MacGregor Records, Los Angeles, California.

Allemande left, coming back to partner with arm around her waist. (Lady does a half left face turn to face same direction as partner.) Gents make a left-hand star and all walk forward counterclockwise in this "star promenade."

It's a heel and toe. You start the music jumpin'
As the ladies roll back can't you see the bustles bumpin'
Oh, you dance through the night as though it were a minute
Your hearts are really in it—The Jessie Polka Dance

As above four lines are called, couples still in star promenade do the Jessie Polka, as follows: With weight on right foot, place left heel to side-front; lean back (count 1). Place left foot beside right and put weight on it (count 2). Place right toe back, lean forward (count 3). Momentarily touch right foot beside left (count 4). Keep weight on left foot, touch right heel forward (count 5). Place right foot beside left and put weight on it (count 6). Touch left toe to side (count 7). Touch left toe in front (count 8). (You may sweep left foot across right instead of touching.) Then do four two-steps still in star and moving counterclockwise (lady rolls right-face to gent behind on last two two-steps).

Repeat two more times.

(Caller cue: side, stand, back touch, front stand, side and cross, two-step, two-step, two-step, and two-step.)

Now that corner maid and as she comes around
Take her in your arms and swing her 'round and 'round
  As ladies roll back the third time, they swing with that gent—original corner.
Then you promenade her home, keep her for your partner
You balance and you swing till the music starts again
  Promenade new partner home and swing. Repeat dance three more times to get original partner back.

MY LITTLE GIRL

Source and music: Record: Old Timer * 8003.
  The following call is sung to the melody:

First couple promenade the outside
Around the outside of the ring *(counterclockwise)*
Those ladies chain right down the center
  Ladies of couples one and three chain.
And chain them back again
Those ladies chain the right-hand couples
  Lady one chains with lady two, and lady three chains with lady four.

And they chain them back again
Those ladies chain the left-hand couples
> *Lady one now chains with lady four, and lady three with lady two.*

And they chain them back again

All around your corner lady .
> *All gents go counterclockwise around their corner ladies.*

See-saw your pretty little taw
Allemande left your left-hand lady

And you grand right and left around the hall
And when you meet, you docey-doe her
> *As you meet your partner in the grand right eight, you go around her counterclockwise right shoulder to right shoulder, back to back, and left shoulder to left shoulder. Then bow.*

And you swing her 'round and 'round *(hip swing)*
Now promenade, just promenade her
Promenade her 'round the town

> *Repeat with couples two, three, and four as the head couples.*

MAÑANA

Source: Revision of original dance by Al McMullen, North Hollywood, California.
Music: Record: Windsor * 7407 and 7104.

INTRODUCTION

Now you honor your chiquita *(partners)*
Give your corner girl a weenk
Allemande left your corner
Grand old right and left, I theenk
Now when you meet your enchilada
Do-sa-do her neat *(partners)*
And promenade the street
> *Everyone sings the chorus while promenading home.*

"Mañana, Mañana, Mañana is good enough for me"

FIGURE I

Vaqueros *(gents)* star across the set
A left-hand swing that girl *(opposite)*
Star back home again real quick
Another left-hand whirl *(partner)*
A right-hand round your corner
Give your own a left-hand swing

* Used by permission of Windsor Records, Temple City, California.

Now promenade that corner girl, and everybody sing
"Mañana, Mañana, Mañana is good enough for me"
Figure ends with gents having original corners for partners.

FIGURE II

Chiquitas *(ladies)* star across the set
A left-hand swing that man *(opposite)*
Star back home and turn your hombre
With the old left hand *(partner)*
A right-hand round your corner
Give your own a left-hand swing
Now promenade your corner girl, and everybody sing
"Mañana, Mañana, Mañana is good enough for me"
Figure ends with gents having original opposites for partners.

BREAK

Allemande left your corner, and pass right by your own
Allemande right your right-hand girl
And leave your own alone
Now allemande left your corner, and give your own a swing
And promenade to Mexico, and everybody sing
"Mañana, Mañana, Mañana is good enough for me"
Figures 1 and 2 and the break are repeated to finish the dance with original partners.

THERE'S A RAINBOW 'ROUND YOUR SHOULDER

Source: Original dance by Randy Stephens, Provo, Utah.
Music: Record: Windsor * 7443.

OPENER, MIDDLE BREAK, AND CLOSER

Walk all around your corners
Bow to your partners all
Gals star right, gents promenade
Go twice around that hall
Now left-hand swing your partners
Once and a half you go
Gents star right, gals promenade
It's twice around you know
Pass her once, pass her again
Allemande left your corners, men
Come back one and promenade
Two-by-two with your pretty little maid
There's a rainbow 'round your shoulder
And it fits you like a glove
The world's all right, we'll dance tonight
The skies are blue above

* Used by permission of Windsor Records, Temple City, California.

Walk all around corners, partners bow, ladies star right while gents promenade counterclockwise outside. On meeting second time, partners turn once and a half with left forearm hold, then gents star right while ladies promenade counterclockwise outside. Partners pass twice, allemande left corners, then partners promenade to home position.

FIGURE

Head gents swing your corners
Now she becomes your own

Concentric circles formation.

Split that ring, go 'round two
And head right back for home
Side gents swing your corners
Now she's your brand new pard
Split that ring, go 'round two
And head for your back yard
Head couples do a right and left through
Side couples do a trail on through
Allemande that corner maid
Now take your own and promenade

There's a rainbow 'round your shoulder
And everyone's in love
We'll swing and sway in the same old way
'Neath skies of blue above

> *Gents one and three swing corners, ending swing with that lady on right side, acquiring a new partner. Head couples pass diagonally through in center, separate around outside of ring, lady to right and gent to left, and return to starting position. Gents two and four duplicate above action ending with all gents having original corners for new partners. Couples one and three right and left through across set. Couples two and four trail on through by passing opposite couple right shoulders in center, after which each lady crosses to her left in front of partner while each gent crosses to his right behind partner. All allemande left corners and promenade new partners back to gents' home positions.*

> *Repeat Figure with head gents active. Repeat opener for middle break. Repeat Figure with side gents active. Repeat Figure with side gents active. Repeat opener for closer.*

POOR LITTLE ROBIN

Source: Original dance by Buzz Brown, San Diego, California.
Music: Record: Old Timer * 8102 and 8103.

OPENER

All around your corner, bow to that pretty little Robin
Now swing that gal around
And then you promenade her
She's your pretty little Robin
Got a teardrop in her eye

FIGURE

Now first and third you ladies chain
Turn 'em boys, you're gone again

> *Touching right hands, passing right shoulders, the head ladies cross to the opposite gentlemen, extend their left hands to the gent's left hands, and the gents turn the ladies counterclockwise to face the ladies on their left.*

Turn and chain to the left side of the ring
Four ladies chain right across the square

> *Ladies form a palm star and turn clockwise to opposite gents.*

Swing that gent and stay right there
Swing that little Robin 'round and 'round *(waist swing)*
(And then it's)
All around your corner *(right shoulders, back to back, left shoulders)*
Bow to that pretty little Robin
Now swing that gal a-round

* Used by permission of Old Timer Record Company, Phoenix, Arizona.

(And then you)
Promenade her, she's your pretty little Robin
Got a teardrop in her eye

BREAK

Four gents star across the square
Turn that Robin, leave her there
Star back home with a left hand 'round your own
Now all join hands in one big ring
Circle left like everything
Circle left go all around the ring
All around your corner
Bow to that pretty little Robin
Now swing that gal a-round
And then you promenade her
She's your pretty little Robin
Got a teardrop in her eye

> *Sequence: Opener, first and third, first and third, break, second and fourth, second and fourth, break.*

CHANTEZ CHANTEZ

Source: Original dance by Fenton "Jonesy" Jones.
Music: Record: MacGregor * 789-B, 790-B (78 rpm); 7895-B, 7905-B (45 rpm).

INTRODUCTION

Walk all around your left-hand lady
See-saw 'round your pretty little taw
Allemande left with the old left hand
Partners right, a right and left grand
Hand over hand around that ring
When you meet your girl
Give 'er a twirl, promenade
Take a little walk with the pretty little maid
Now you're home—balance out
Everybody swing

FIGURE

Now one and three lead to the right
Circle half, it's fun
Dive through, California whirl
> *The ladies turn under their partners' right arms, as they exchange positions and also reverse their line of direction.*
Split the sides—go 'round just one
Opposites right, box the gnat
> *The lady executes a right-face turn under the gent's right arm.*
Star right in the middle and then

* **Used by permission of MacGregor Records, Los Angeles, California.**

The dancers form a right-hand star in the center of the set.
Corners left, box the flea
> *Like box the gnat, but with the left hand.*

See-saw 'round this honey bee
Balance out, step right up and swing a brand new wren
Allemande left, the ladies star *(palm star)*
The gents go 'round the ring
Reverse the star, reverse the ring
Pass 'er once, you're gone again, we'll meet again *(original partner)*
Box the gnat, the gents star left *(go)*
Once around and then *(you go)*
Give 'er a twirl, promenade
Walk right along with the pretty little maid
Now you're home, balance out
Swing her high and low
> *Repeat figure for sides.*

RIDIN' OLD PAINT

Source: Original dance by Fenton "Jonesy" Jones.
Music: Record: MacGregor * 789-A.

FIGURE

Walk all around your left-hand lady
> *Right shoulder back to back.*

See-saw 'round your pretty little baby
> *Left shoulder back to back.*

Join your hands, let's circle 'round the floor
The first old couple rip and snort
Go down the center, tie 'em up short
Break at the foot, form two lines of four
> *Without releasing hand holds, couple one goes down the center and through the arch formed by couple three. Couple one then separates, the gent to the left, the lady to the right, and couple three releases joined hands and the dancers form two lines, facing the center.*

Forward eight, come back with you
Bend your line, square through
Do a right, a left, a right, a left
> *The inside couples act as a hinge, the ends walk forward to form two lines of four. The gents extend right hands to the right hands of their original opposite ladies, then pass through and remain facing out. Then the gents face left, the ladies right, and repeat the movement with their original corners using the left hand. They are half-way through. Repeat the movement; the gents retain hand holds with their original corners.*

Face your corners, promenade
You've got yourselves a brand new maid

* Used by permission of MacGregor Records, Los Angeles, California.

Ridin' old Paint—Ridin' old Paint
And leading old Bald

> *Repeat the figure three more times.*

> *Note: The "square through" was originated by Bill Hansen of Los Angeles, California, and can be executed in many patterns. One of the patterns is used in this call.*

SAMBA SQUARE

Source: Original dance by Johnny Velotta, Hollywood, California.
Music: Record: Windsor * 7442.
Basic step: Samba (see page 213).

OPENER, MIDDLE BREAK, AND CLOSER
Walk all around that corner girl
And pass behind your own
See-saw round the right-hand gal
Come back and swing at home
When you're through with swingin'
Gents star left around that square
A right hand 'round your partner
When you find her standin' there
Allemande your corner lady
Then you do-sa-do at home
Allemande left just once again
Then promenade your own
Well, promenade your Cuban queen right back to ol' Havana
It's home you go and step up, Joe
And swing until mañana

> *Walk all around corners, pass left shoulders with partners, see-saw right-hand ladies starting left shoulders, swing partners. Gents star left full around square, turn partners with right forearm hold, allemande left corners, do-sa-do partners, allemande left corners again, promenade with partners full around square, swing briefly at home.*

FIGURE
First and third go to the right
And circle half around
Dive on through and star by the left
About three-quarters 'round
A right hand 'round your corner
And a left hand 'round your pal
Then promenade with the corner girl
Ya got a brand new pal
Well, let 'er go, the gals move on
The men will right-hand star
Pass her once and when you meet

The gents reverse that star
Pick 'em up—star promenade
And you walk along back home
And when you reach Havana
Balance out and swing your own

Couples one and three go to right-hand couples, circle just half around until couples two and four are back to back in center. Couples one and three dive under arch made by two and four. While couples two and four return to home positions, couples one and three star left in center, walking three-fourths around set to original corners. Turn corners with right forearm, turn partners with left forearm, promenade corners until next call. As ladies continue to promenade counterclockwise around set, gents turn left face into a right-hand star and walk clockwise in center of set; new partners (original corners) pass each other once; then, as they meet the second time, gents turn left face to make a left-hand star in center, picking up new partner for star promenade at the same time. Partners star promenade to gents' home position where they balance out at arm's length and swing briefly.

Repeat figure with head couples again active. Repeat opener for middle break. Repeat figure with side couples active. Repeat figure with side couples again active. Repeat opener for closer.

Double circle facing clockwise.

SWEET JENNIE LEE

Source: Original dance by Bob Johnson, Phoenix, Arizona.
Music: Record: Dash * 2501-A, 2501-B.

INTRODUCTION, BREAK, AND ENDING

You bow, the gents star left
One time is not too far
Your partner right hand 'round
A wrong way thar
Throw in the clutch, here we go
All turn back, pass your own
> *Gents reverse the star, girls reverse the ring.*

Your corners allemande
Go right and left grand
And now go hand over hand around that ring
Until you meet your maid
You do-sa-do your honey, promenade
> *Everybody join in the chorus.*

Sweet Jennie Lee
From sunny Tennessee
She's swingin' now with me
Sweet Jennie Lee

DANCE PATTERN

Your corner do-sa-do
See-saw that girl you know
Then face your corner Jane
And all eight chain
> *Right to the corner lady; pull her by. A left to the next and curtsy; turn this lady to face the center of the set. In this movement each gent will progress one fourth around the set and will end with his original opposite lady.*

Girls star you know
It's one full time you go
To an allemande thar, gents back up, a right-hand star
And then you shoot that star, go right and left grand
Around that big ole ring
You promenade your honey and you sing
Sweet Jennie Lee
From sunny Tennessee
She's swingin' now with me
Sweet Jennie Lee
> *Sequence: Introduction, two changes, break, two changes, ending.*

* Used by permission of Dash Records, Phoenix, Arizona.

HONEYCOMB (Singing Square)

Source: Original dance by Ruth Stillion, Arcata, California.
Music: Record: Windsor * 7461, 7161.

OPENER, MIDDLE BREAK, AND CLOSER

Gents star left, go once around
Take your girl with an arm around
Star promenade and . . . what then? . . .
Back out and the girls sweep in
Star by the right in the usual way
Four little ladies roll away
Gents star right, the girls turn back
Just once around (and do that)
Allemande left with the corner lady
Round the ring you roam (to meet a) Hank o' hair and a piece of
       bone
Go walk 'n talk with . . . Honeycomb
Oh Honeycomb, won'tcha be my baby
Honeycomb be my own
Well, swing 'er neat, she's kinda sweet
Like Honeycomb . . .

> *Gents star left full around and pick up partner in a star promenade. Gents back out and ladies sweep in with a full turn around ending with ladies in center with right-hand star. Ladies roll left face across in front of gents to outside of set, and gents star right in center. Ladies turn left face out of star and backtrack in counterclockwise direction. Pass partner once and immediately allemande left with original corner; do grand right and left; promenade partner to home position.*

FIGURE

Gals to the middle, back to back
Gents buzz around the outside track
Like a honeybee, lookin' for a home
Turn a left hand 'round your own
Corners by the right, it's a catch-all-eight,
Back by the left and don't be late
Ladies star three-quarters round . . . (turn a)
Left hand full around

Gents to the right and do-sa-do
Same little lady—promeno
She's a hank o' hair and a piece of bone
Go walk 'n' talk with . . . Honeycomb
Balance home and do-sa-do
She's your honeybee, you know
Then swing and whirl
A pretty little girl—like Honeycomb . . .

* Used by permission of Windsor Records, Temple City, California.

Ladies stand back to back in center, gents promenade counter-clockwise around outside of set. Turn partner left, do a catch-all-eight with corner by turning half-way around with right, back with left forearm full around. Ladies star three-fourths around inside of set to original opposite, turn with a left forearm swing, gents progress to next lady counterclockwise around set, original corner, to do-sa-do, taking the same lady for a new partner to promenade full around set to home position.

Sequence: Opener, figure twice, middle break, figure twice, closer.

SLINGING HASH

Source and Music: Record: Windsor * 7406.

FIGURE 1—"HOT TIME IN THE OLD TOWN TONIGHT"

First couple right and you circle four hands 'round
Pick up two more and make it six hands 'round
Pick up two more and make it eight hands 'round
There'll be a hot time in the old town tonight
Allemande left with the lady on your left *(corner)*
Allemande right with the lady on your right *(right-hand lady)*
Allemande left with the lady on your left *(corner)*
And a grand old right and left around the ring
And when you meet your honey, do-sa-do around
Take her in your arms and swing her off the ground
Then you promenade around with the cutest gal in town
There'll be a hot time in the old town tonight

FIGURE 2—"MY PRETTY GIRL"

Second couple promenade—around the outside
Around the outside of the ring
Side ladies *(two and four)* chain right down the center
And you chain them back again
Side ladies chain the right-hand couples
And you chain them back again
Side ladies chain the left-hand couples
And you chain them back again

FIGURE 3—"ALABAMA JUBILEE"

Four little ladies promenade inside the ring
Go back to your partner and give him a swing
Do-sa-do with the corner girl
Bow to your partner and you give her a whirl

* Used by permission of Windsor Records, Temple City, California.

Four gents promenade inside the hall
Back to your partner and do-sa-do all
Give the corner girl a swing and take that girl around the ring
To the Alabama Jubilee . . . whooee, to the Alabama Jubilee!
Figure ends with gents having original corners for partners.

FIGURE 4—"WABASH CANNONBALL"

Third old couple lead to the right, circle four a while
On to the next, pick up two and watch those ladies smile
On to the next and pick up two, and listen to my call
You circle eight and don't be late
On the Wabash Cannonball
Now all four couples separate, go 'round the outside ring
*Ladies promenade to right inside the set while gents promenade
to left on the outside.*
Meet your corner with a right-hand 'round
Your own with a left-hand swing
*Pass by starting partner, meet corner with right forearm swing,
give partner left forearm swing full around.*
The corner right and flip her in front
Now listen to my call
Couple up cars and head out south
On the Wabash Cannonball.
*Give corner right forearm swing half around, giving her a flip
to turn her slightly on releasing so that she faces counterclock-
wise around the set in front of gent. Promenade single file with
left hands, taking the left elbow of person in front, churning
like a locomotive drive rod. Continue full turn around to gent's
home position. Men now have original opposites for partners.*

FIGURE 5—"YOU CALL EVERYBODY DARLING"

First and third lead to the right and circle-o
Twice around in a pretty little ring you go
Now break at the heads and form two lines
Forward and back, you're doing fine
Right and left through and over you go
Now hurry, don't be slow
Right and left back with your darling
Chain those ladies right across the line
Now take that gal back home
Two side ladies *(two and four)* chain across *(but don't chain back)*
Swing your little darling evermore
End figure with original right-hand ladies for partners.

FIGURE 6—"RED WING"

Oh, the fourth couple right and you circle half
Inside couple arch
And you dip and dive and away you go,
The inside high and the outside low
Hurry, hurry, hurry let's go

Threes facing threes formation.

Over and then below
Then dip right through to the lonesome two *(couple two)*
And circle half-way round
Now dive to the next and circle half *(to couple one)*
The inside couple arch
And you dip and dive and away you go,
The inside high and the outside low
Hurry, hurry, hurry let's go
Over and then below
Now you're through so what do you do . . . why, everybody swing

FIGURE 7—"OH, JOHNNY"

All join hands and you circle the ring *(to the right)*
Stop where you are, give your honey a swing
Now you swing that girl behind you *(corner)*
And you swing your own . . . if you've got time to
Allemande left with the lady on your left *(corner)*
And do-sa-do your own
Now you all promenade—that corner maid
Singing "Oh, Johnny—Oh, Johnny—Oh!"

End dance with original partner.

178   Square Dances

THAT OLD BLACK MAGIC

Source: Original dance by Randy Stephens, Provo, Utah.
Music: Record: Windsor * 7160.

OPENER, MIDDLE BREAK, AND CLOSER

You join your hands and circle 'round the ring
Your corner's left, and partner's right hand swing
Now all four ladies promenade the land
Hey—box the gnat, and do a right and left grand

Those icy fingers up and down the line
You promenade the little gal you find
Promenade your pet, and you're bound to get
That old black magic called fun.

> *All join hands and circle left, turn corners with left, turn part-ners with right, four ladies promenade counterclockwise inside set back to partner, partners box the gnat and do the usual right and left grand, meeting across set for a full promenade back to home position.*

FIGURE

The heads to the right and circle round the track
Break to a line, go forward up and back
Now right and left through, and face 'em down the lane
Let's "dixie chain," and then the two ladies chain

Now all join hands and circle 'round the hall
Do a left allemande, then promenade your taw
Promenade that line, and you're sure to find
That old black magic called fun

> *Couples one and three go to couple on their right, join hands, circle once around, breaking to a line of four. The lines of four go forward and back, then right and left through across the lines, ending the courtesy turn to face down each line, couple one facing two and couple three facing four. Couples facing do a "dixie chain" with the ladies leading; ladies pass each other touching right hands; ladies pass a man touching left hands; ladies then proceed in same direction around set to pass another lady, touching right hands as in the usual two-ladies chain while two gents pass each other touching right hands; gents then give a courtesy turn to the next lady coming their way, gaining a new partner. Tuᴐ gents will have original corners as new partners, two gents will have original right-hand ladies as partners. All join hands and circle left. Allemande left corners, promenade new partners full around set to home posi-tion.*
>
> *Sequence: Opener, figure twice for heads, middle break, figure twice for sides, closer.*

* Used by permission of Windsor Records, Temple City, California.

Square Dances   **179**

SOMEBODY GOOFED

Source: Original dance by Ruth Stillion, Coos Bay, Oregon.
Music: Record: Windsor * 7140.

FIGURE 1

The head two, a right and left through
Sides you do the same
The head two, a right and left back
Sides do it again
All four couples right and left
Grand around the ring
You meet your maid and promenade,
And everybody sing . . .

FIGURE 2

Allemande left, the ladies star, the gentlemen promenade
Allemande left, the gentlemen star, the ladies promenade
Allemande left the corner girl, do-sa-do your own
Find your right-hand lady, boys, and promenade her home . . .

FIGURE 3

Swing the one across the hall
Wink at the corner gal
Star right back and turn your own
A left hand 'round your pal
Do-sa-do your corners all
Balance to your taw
Find the one who winked at you
And promenade the hall . . .

FIGURE 4

The four gents lead to the right, balance to that gal
Pass the one behind you, a left to the corner—pal
Star right across the set, a left hand 'round her there
Find the one you balanced to, and promenade the square . . .

FIGURE 5

Swing the corner lady, swing her round and round
Swing the next one down the line, bounce her up and down
Go back home and swing your own, now listen to the call
Find the one you haven't swung, and promenade the hall . . .

FIGURE 6

Allemande left the corners, then do an allemande thar
Go right and left and then the gentlemen, form a right-hand star
Shoot the star, go all the way, docey corners all
Find the one you had in the star, and promenade the hall . . .

* Used by permission of Windsor Records, Temple City, California.

FIGURE 7

Bow low to your partner, swing the corner high
Allemande left in the usual way
And pass your partner by
Do-sa-do the next one, she ought to be your own
Find the one who passed you by and promenade her home . . .

MARIANNE

Source: Original square dance by Dick Leger, Providence, Rhode Island.
Music: Record: Folkraft * 1282.

INTRODUCTION

Four little ladies chain across
    (You turn 'em with your left hand)
You chain those ladies back again
    (You turn your Marianne)
Dos-a-dos your corner—Dos-a-dos your own
Bow to your corner—but swing your own
    (Hurry up now!)

CHORUS

All day, all night, Marianne
    (Promenade 'em)
Down by the seaside along the sand
    (Sing it)
Even little children like Marianne
    (Swing 'em)
Down by the seaside along the sand
    (Square your sets now)

PATTERN

Head two couples pass through—around just one you go
Go down the middle and cross trail
Around just one you know
You box the gnat at home
Four gents a left-hand star around
Now go back home and dos-a-dos
Your corner swing *(Don't rush me)*

CHORUS

All day, all night, Marianne, *etc.*

Head couples repeat Pattern and Chorus.

Repeat entire dance, starting with introduction, with side couples leading.

* Used by permission of Folkraft Records, Newark, New Jersey.

10

Soft

Shoe

and

Tap

Dancing

During the nineteenth century, dance began to play an increasingly important role in the recreational activities of Americans. As we have seen, square dancing became popular, with all regions contributing new ideas to its development. It was not, however, a style of dance original with Americans. As individualism grew, a need for an original dance form grew with it, a dance that would be an expression of the many cultures of the new nation.

Just as the white settlers brought their music and dances from Europe, the Negro slaves brought their tribal songs and dances from Africa. These people had been taught to sing and dance for each important event in life, and they believed that the arts were half magic and would bring success in any endeavor. The slaves sang Christian hymns to pagan rhythms, and these became our heritage of Negro spirituals. They imitated the dances of their masters and added movements of their own. The white people in turn imitated the Negroes, and thus was developed the minstrel show. The use of blackface theatrically was recorded in Massachusetts as early as 1799. By 1840, it had assumed a dominant role on the American stage.

From the minstrel show came the first major innovation for dance·in the United States—soft shoe and tap dancing. The difference between soft shoe and tap dancing lies basically in the type of shoes worn. Soft shoe is done with soft-soled shoes, whereas tap is done with metal taps on the heels and toes of the shoes.

As this dance form became more and more popular, entertainers borrowed steps and styles from other folk and social dances, and, through personal invention, expanded their repertoires. River showboats and traveling vaudeville troupes spread the minstrel show, with all its variations and refinements, throughout the land.

By the beginning of the twentieth century, tap dancing was a must for Broadway musicals. It contributed greatly to the rise of commercial dance studios and became a part of the school curriculum. And it affected recreational dance patterns. Social dancing, popular music, and musical comedy as·we know them today are in kinship with tap dancing. Modern jazz dancing is its grandchild. Its impact has been felt throughout the world.

APPROACHES TO TAP DANCE INSTRUCTION

Tap dancing has developed many variations from the first minstrel shows to the present time. The type of tap dance for a particular performance is governed by the musical accompaniment, the number of dancers, the costumes, and the setting. The mood is set by the music; costumes and settings can further emphasize mood. The projection of the dancer through movement, pattern, and rhythm can make the finished product either "much ado about nothing" or a work of art.

PROJECTION

Frequently the choreographer uses fairly simple steps to compose a tap dance. He knows that the quality of the performance will be determined by the ability of the dancer. The secret lies not in the arrangement of the steps, but in the manner in which they are danced. For example, the same tap routine used by a professional dancer can be taught to a beginner. A layman watching both dancers would find it difficult to believe the actual routine was the same. The difference would lie in the projection of each dancer's personality, his style, his shadings of rhythm, and his patterns of movement. Much of this is acquired through training and experience.

However, the time required for mastering these aspects can be shortened if the need for individual projection is emphasized with the beginning student.

Often an instructor is excessively concerned with teaching tap steps to the student. He performs a step in front of the student over and over until the student learns by repetition. The result is parrot-like. The student may not understand what he is doing. He has little conception of either step construction or rhythmic pattern. The instructor may use this method of instruction because he is unable to break a tap step down to its barest essentials. On the other hand, he may be capable of teaching the step by fundamentals but elects to withhold this information from the student. The result is that the student is more or less dependent on the instructor and must continue taking tap lessons. Therefore, the student hesitates to experiment with personal innovations in styling and choreography.

The mastery of basic tap fundamentals permits the student to concentrate on rhythm and styling of presentation. As he becomes more sure of himself, he can engage in personal choreographic efforts. Then, and only then, can he achieve the major objectives of recreational dance—self-expression and creativeness through the coordination of mind and body.

FUNDAMENTALS

The student must know the fundamentals of tap dancing if he is to understand what he is doing. When he has mastered the fundamentals and understands how they are combined and altered to make up steps, the student is better qualified to engage in personal innovation. Styling and rhythm can become such a part of these basic fundamentals that they carry over into complete steps and routines.

Every instructor must devise the method of presentation of fundamentals that best suits his personal needs and those of his class. The presentation suggested in this book is designed for the novice teacher and follows a plan of progression based on degree of acquired skills. Caution must be exercised by the teacher to prevent the means from becoming ends in themselves. The sooner the student can be started on combining these fundamentals into an actual tap step that will become part of a complete routine, the more effective the lesson will be.

The first concerns in the first lesson should be balance and coordination. The student will need some form of support for balance during the first lesson. With small children, support may be needed for several lessons. If the lesson is conducted in an equipped dance studio, have the students spaced out, standing perpendicular to the bar. They may support themselves by placing the left hand on the bar. If a studio bar is not available, the left hand may be placed on the back of a chair; chairs may be spaced along the walls. If neither chairs nor bars are available, have students place their left palms against the wall at a comfortable height. After the tap fundamentals have been learned, eliminate these supports for balance; otherwise the student will become dependent on them. Students may then be placed in line, horseshoe, or circle formation, as determined by the size of the class.

It is advisable to teach tap fundamentals by using standard tap terminology and correct rhythm count. Several of the large national associations of dance teachers have attempted to standardize tap terminology so that the tap student in a western town will learn the terminology used by professionals in New York. Until this effort was made by associations such as the Dance Masters of America and the Dance Educators of America, it was not uncommon for a specific tap fundamental to be known by a half dozen names. Differences date back to the days of vaudeville, when hoofers gave their own names to steps for which they hoped to become famous. The use of standard terminology avoids confusion and offers a short cut that enables students to learn faster.

Tap fundamentals can be divided into two classifications, stationary and progressive. The former are those that are danced in a confined area; the latter are those that move the dancer forward. Stationary fundamentals are taught with the student using some form of support as outlined above. The progressive fundamentals are usually taught in a line or circle, progressing forward.

Stationary tap fundamentals:

1. *Tap*—extend the leg so that only the toe touches the floor; by bending the ankle, raise the toe from the floor and let it fall to make a tap sound. This is usually repeated evenly for a specific number of rhythmic counts.

2. *Toe tap*—with one foot perpendicular to the floor, tap the tip of the toe behind the other foot.

3. *Brush*—hold one foot with bent knee off the floor and behind the other foot; make an arc by moving the foot to the opposite direction, ending with straight knee and foot extended off the floor. Only the ball of the foot touches the floor as it passes parallel to the other foot.

4. *Brush tap*—add a tap to a brush. If the brush progresses from forward to back, use a toe tap instead of a tap.

5. *Brush tap down*—add a step in place to the brush tap; after the step, the opposite foot is free to do a brush tap down.

6. *Shuffle*—brush forward and snap the toe back quickly off the floor by raising the bent knee. Take care that the heel does not touch the floor.

7. *Shuffle down*—add a step in place to the shuffle; after the step, the opposite foot is free to do a shuffle down.

8. *Shuffle heel*—do a shuffle with one foot, raise the heel of the opposite foot supporting body weight, and release to the floor.

9. *Shuffle heel tap*—add a toe tap to the shuffle heel.

10. *Shuffle hop*—do a shuffle, then *hop* on opposite foot supporting body weight.

11. *Shuffle hop down*—add a step in place to the shuffle hop; after the step, the opposite foot is free to do a shuffle hop down.

12. *Ball change*—step on the ball of the foot, while raising the heel off the floor; transfer weight to opposite foot, which steps in place. (*Note:* Most people at some time have had a cut or bruised heel. They "favor" the heel by walking on the ball of the injured foot; the action involved in a ball change is similar. Students may practice by walking around the room "favoring" a heel so that they may learn this fundamental quickly.)

13. *Shuffle ball change*—do a shuffle, then a ball change.

14. *Waltz clog*—step in place with one foot taking the weight; do a shuffle ball change with the opposite foot. (*Note:* A 3/4 time signature is

usually used for this fundamental. If 4/4 music is used, add a hop on the foot supporting body weight for the extra rhythm count.)

Progressive tap fundamentals:

1. *Flap*—brush foot from back into a forward step, taking the weight; reverse on opposite foot. (*Note:* The action involved is similar to slapping the foot while brushing it. Many students confuse a shuffle and a flap because the two fundamentals sound much alike. The difference is that after a shuffle the foot is off the floor and after a flap it is on the floor supporting body weight.)

2. *Toe heel*—spank the floor with the toe, taking the weight on the ball of that foot; release the raised heel to the floor. Progress forward by reversing the toe heel on the opposite foot.

A tap routine finish.

3. *Flap heel*—brush forward and add a toe heel; reverse.

4. *Down hop*—step forward and hop, while raising the opposite foot off the floor in the back; reverse.

5. *Flap hop*—add a hop to a flap while raising the opposite foot from the floor in the rear; reverse.

6. *Down ball change*—step forward and ball change from the back; reverse. (*Note:* This can also be done in a stationary position: step to the side and add a ball change from the side; reverse.)

7. *Flap ball change*—add a ball change to a flap; reverse.

8. *Cramp roll*—flap forward on ball of the foot, keeping heel raised off the floor during a toe heel on opposite foot, then release raised heel to the floor; reverse.

Soft Shoe and Tap Dancing   **187**

In tap dancing, the student must learn to execute fundamentals and steps with equal proficiency of both feet. In addition, many fundamentals must be danced forward, sideward, and backward. It is therefore advisable to teach fundamentals in such a manner that the student may acquire sufficient experience in using both feet in the various desired directions. These fundamentals should be taught with musical accompaniment. The student must learn to listen to the music so that his tap steps will coincide with the correct count for the music.

If the students use some form of balanced support during practice of stationary fundamentals, a half turn toward the barre, wall, or chair upon completion of one exercise will permit execution of the exercise on the opposite foot. If line, horseshoe, or circle formation is used, a step in place will free the opposite foot for performing the reverse of the exercise.

The following procedures are suggested:

Stationary:

1. *Tap*—R (right) foot fwd (forward) 8 x's (eight times); R to R side 8 x's; R toe tap bk (back) 8 x's; R to R side 7 x's, step in place on 8th count or make half turn to face opposite direction taking weight on R foot. Using a 4/4 time signature, each tap requires one beat; therefore, 8 taps require 2 measures of music. The entire pattern takes 8 measures or one phrase of music. Following the step in place or the half turn, reverse the pattern using the L (left) foot. Ct: full (one full count of music).

2. *Brush*—brush R fwd 4 x's, brush R to R side 4 x's, brush R bk 4 x's, brush R to R side 3 x's, make a half turn or step in place. Take 2 counts on each brush; pattern requires 8 measures. Reverse pattern by using L foot following step in place or half turn by R foot. Ct: full.

3. *Brush tap*—using R foot, brush tap fwd 4 x's, to R side 4 x's, back 4 x's, to R side 3 x's, step in place or make a half turn. Pattern requires 8 measures. Reverse, beginning with L foot. Ct: 1-2.

4. *Brush tap down*—alternate feet RLRLRLRL. 8 x's requires 8 measures. Ct: 1-2-3-4 (hold 4).

5. *Shuffle*—using R foot, shuffle 8 x's fwd, 8 x's to R side, 8 x's bk, 7 x's to R side, step in place or make a half turn. Requires 8 measures. Reverse, starting L foot. Ct: &1.

6. *Shuffle down*—alternate feet RLRLRLRL. 8 x's requires 8 measures. Ct: 1&2.

7. *Shuffle heel*—R fwd 4 x's, R side 4 x's, R bk 4 x's, R side 3 x's, step in place or make a half turn. Requires 8 measures. Reverse, starting L foot. Ct: &1-2.

8. *Shuffle heel tap*—do 7 x's with R executing shuffle in front and toe tap in bk, step in place or make a half turn. Requires 8 measures. Reverse, starting L foot. Ct: &1&2.

9. *Shuffle hop*—R shuffle fwd 4 x's, to R side 4 x's, bk 4 x's, to R side 3 x's, step in place or make a half turn. Requires 8 measures. Reverse, starting L foot. Ct: &1-2.

10. *Shuffle hop down*—alternate feet RLRLRLRL. 8 x's requires 8 measures. Ct: &1&2.

11. *Ball change*—starting with R each time, 4 x's fwd, 4 x's to R side, 4 x's bk, 3 x's to R side, step in place or make a half turn. Requires 8 measures. Reverse, starting each with L foot. Ct: &1.

12. *Shuffle ball change*—do 3 x's starting R with shuffle fwd and ball change bk; add one shuffle down taking weight on R foot. Requires 2 measures. Reverse, starting with L, repeat starting with R, reverse starting with L. Entire pattern requires 8 measures. Ct: &1&2.

Progressive:

1. *Flap*—progress fwd with flap 8 x's, alternating feet RLRLRLRL. Requires 8 measures. Ct: &1.

2. *Toe heel*—progress fwd with toe heel 8 x's; alternate feet for 8 measures. Ct: 1-2.

3. *Flap heel*—progress fwd with flap heel, alternating feet for 8 measures. Ct: &1-2.

4. *Down hop*—progress fwd with down hop, alternating feet for 8 measures. Ct: 1-2.

5. *Flap hop*—progress fwd with flap hop, alternating feet for 8 measures. Ct: &1-2.

6. *Down ball change*—progress fwd with down ball change, alternating feet for 8 measures. Ct: 1&2.

7. *Flap ball change*—progress fwd with flap ball change, alternating feet for 8 measures. Ct: &1&2.

8. *Cramp roll*—progress fwd with cramp rolls, alternating feet for 8 measures. Ct: &1&a2.

CONSTRUCTING STEPS FROM FUNDAMENTALS

Tap steps as part of an entire routine can be constructed from these basic fundamentals. Both the novice tap teacher and the beginning tap student should experiment with choreography utilizing these fundamentals. A little practice with such a procedure builds self-confidence and makes the teacher a better instructor and the student a more interested pupil. Both will find enjoyment in combining the endless possibilities of these fundamentals.

The following is a beginning tap routine based on tap fundamentals:

Entrance—4 measures:

Progress L to R stage, facing R stage; swing opposite hands.

1	2						8
toe	heel	alternate	LRLRLR				down (face audience)
R	R						L

Step 1—8 measures:

Facing audience, swing opposite hand fwd to point to foot doing tap.

1	2	3	4	5	6	7	8
brush	tap	down	(hold)	brush	tap	down	(hold)
R	R	R		L	L	L	

1		2.	3–4	5–6	7	8
toe	tap (bk of L)	down	reverse	repeat	down	(hold)
R		R	L	R	L	

Repeat entire step.

Soft Shoe and Tap Dancing **189**

Step II—8 measures:

Facing audience, swing opposite hand fwd, pushing flat palm to coincide with tap of opposite foot.

1&	2	3&4	5&6	7&8
Shuffle	down	reverse	repeat	reverse
R	R	L	R	L

1	2		3–4	5–6	7		8
tap fwd	down (in place)		reverse	repeat	down (in place)		hold
R	R		L	R	L		

Repeat entire step.

Step III—8 measures:

Facing front on the first four measures of this step, make small clockwise circles with stretched palm toward audience.

&1	&	2		&7	8	
shuffle	ball	change	3 x's	shuffle	down	—2 meas.
R	R	L		R	R	

Reverse on L	—2 meas.
Repeat on R, making complete turn R	—2 meas.
Reverse on L, making complete turn L	—2 meas.

Step IV—8 measures:

Facing audience, raise wrist in opposition to foot doing shuffle on first four measures; sway both arms to side doing flap during last four measures.

&1	&	2	&3&4	&5&6	&7&8	
shuffle	hop	down	reverse	repeat	reverse	—4 meas.
R	L	R	LRL	RLR	LRL	

1	&	2	3&4	5&6	7		8	
down	ball	change	reverse	repeat	down (in place)		hold	—4 meas.
R	L	R	LRL	RLR	L			

Step V—8 measures:

Face R stage and progress R for first two measures; face audience for next two measures. Sway hands in opposition to lead foot.

&1	2	&3-4	&5-6	7		8	
flap	heel	reverse	repeat	down (in place)		hold	—2 meas.
R	R	LL	RR	L			

Turn R, facing front on clap of hands:

1	2		3-4	5-6	7	8	
tap fwd	down (feet together)		reverse	repeat	clap hands	hold	—2 meas.
R	R		LL	RR			

Reverse entire step to L, beginning L foot	—4 meas.

Step VI—8 measures:

Face audience and progress to R diagonal, swaying hands in opposition to lead foot.

&1	&2	&3	4		&5	&6	&7	8	
flap	flap	flap	clap hands		flap	flap	flap	hold	—2 meas.
R	L	R			L	R	L		

&1		&	2		&3&4	&5&6	&7
shuffle (fwd)		heel	tap (bk)		reverse	repeat	shuffle
R		L	R		LRL	RLR	R
8							
down (in place)							—2 meas.
R							

Reverse entire step to L diagonal, beginning L foot   —4 meas.

Step VII—8 measures:

Face audience and drop shoulder, pointing index finger to foot, doing toe heel (in place) for meas. 3, 4, 7, 8.

&1	&	2	&3&4	&5&6	&7&8	
shuffle	toe	heel	reverse	repeat	reverse	—2 meas.
R	R	R	LLL	RRR	LLL	

1	2	3	4	5	6	7		8	
toe	heel	toe	heel	toe	heel	down (in place)		hold	—2 meas.
R	R	L	L	R	R	L			

Repeat entire step, beginning with R foot   —4 meas.

Step VIII—8 measures:

Progress in small, complete circle to R during first four measures; progress to R stage as exit during last four measures. Sway arms in opposition to lead foot; extend R hand to audience and bow head on final count for ending dance.

&1	&	2	&3&4	&5&6	&7&8	
flap	ball	change	reverse	repeat	reverse	—2 meas.
R	L	R	LRL	RLR	LRL	

&1	2	&3-4	&5-6	7	8	
flap	heel	reverse	repeat	down	hold	—2 meas.
R	R	LL	RR	L		

Repeat first two measures   —2 meas.

&1	2	&3-4	5		
flap	heel	reverse	down (to R, face audience)		
R	R	LL	R		
6			7	8	
toe tap (bk of R)			extend hand	hold	—2 meas.
L			R		

STYLING

The tap dancer must dance with his entire body. The basic rule for any kind of dance is *let the body move in harmony with the feet.* The movement is natural and is accentuated when the hands and arms are moved in opposition to the lead foot. The use of hands should be a buildup to coincide with the stress of a specific step. Tap dancing revolves around the fundamental principle of sound and rhythm. Gestures, gimmicks, and accouterments should harmonize with, rather than detract from, the rhythmic pattern.

The personality of the dancer is projected through his rendition of the tap routine. He must learn that one smile is worth two tap steps. The successful tap dancer dances with his entire body and gives every appearance of enjoying himself to the utmost. His steps are his vehicle. His style is his rendition. His smile is his personal enjoyment—and that spells the goal of recreation!

11

Social

Dance

Social dance as it is known today is an outgrowth of primitive folk and round dances. Its exact origin is not known. Similarities to its present-day form may be traced to about the beginning of the Reformation.

Sixteenth-century social dances were group dances similar to the round dances of today. During the eighteenth century, when the spirit of individualism swept the world, various forms of social dance became popular.

The earliest forms of social dance were waltzes. The volta of Italy, the minuet of France, the Führung of Germany and the Ländler of Austria were the parents of the eighteenth-century waltz. In its infancy, the waltz resembled adagio dancing of today. It was frequently viewed with much disfavor.

Early in the nineteenth century the galop, which became the polka, had its origin in Europe. It, too, was considered indecent and was looked upon with considerable disfavor. The French cancan, the grandparent of today's chorus-girl routines, had its origin shortly after that of the polka.

193

The latter part of the nineteenth century saw the beginning of the two-step, the cakewalk, the maxixe, the bunny hug, the grizzly bear, the turkey trot, and the one-step. Ragtime music began about 1900.

Early in the twentieth century, the tango, the fox trot, and various forms of the waltz became extremely popular.

Shortly after World War I, the shimmy and other forms of jazz dancing became popular. This craze was followed by the Charleston, the black bottom, the rhumba, and marathon dances during the twenties.

During the thirties the most popular kind of social dance was swing, with its many variations such as the big apple, the lindy hop and the New Yorker. In the forties the conga, the samba, and the mambo appeared.

After World War II the bunny hop, the cha cha cha, the calypso, the merengue, rock 'n roll, the twist, and the stomp became the major forms of recreational dance.

FUNDAMENTAL TECHNIQUES

The full aesthetic value in recreational dance cannot be realized without the mastery of several basic fundamentals such as poise, relaxation, and ability to move harmoniously with others. This last fundamental is involved in the ability to lead and to follow.

Posture. Bad posture makes aesthetic dancing impossible. Gravity, lack of muscle tone, boredom, and life's ever-present burdens are constantly pulling the human torso out of alignment. Kinesthetic awareness is essential to maintaining good posture. A person looks better and operates more efficiently when he sits, stands, and moves in a tall position.

Leaning. In dance, a person must lean with his body, in the direction in which he intends to move, before he moves his feet.

Leg movements. The moving leg should always swing forward from the hip. The toes should be pointed straight ahead. The knee of the supporting leg should be slightly flexed, and the weight should be balanced on the balls of the feet. People who carry their weight on their heels are heavy dancers; those who carry their weight forward on the balls of their feet are light dancers. The degree to which the supporting knee is bent determines the length of the step.

Upper part of body. One should carry the chin slightly raised, chest up, abdomen in, hips forward, and buttocks tucked under. This type of posture aids one in developing an elastic step. The arms and hands should be relaxed.

DANCE ETIQUETTE

1. Dress appropriately for the situation.
2. Be sure you are clean and that your clothes are clean and odorless.
3. Learn to dance smoothly.
4. Move counterclockwise around the floor.
5. Don't be a show-off.

6. Smile, be pleasant, and don't move around on the dance floor as if you had a stomach-ache. If you are sick, stay home.

7. Ask the lady, "May I have this dance?" Don't say "You want to dance?" "Do you have a dance?" "Let's dance," etc.

8. Apologize if you bump someone or if you step on someone's foot.

9. At the end of the dance, always escort your partner to her seat and thank her for dancing with you.

10. Ladies, don't hang on to your partner; carry your own weight.

11. Don't pump your arms up and down while dancing.

12. Ladies, don't refuse someone who asks you to dance and then dance with someone else to that same piece of music.

13. Learn to glide smoothly on the floor.

14. Look alive; don't move like a dead fish.

15. Don't pop your gum.

16. Don't sing or whistle; don't carry on a conversation while dancing if you can't stay in step with the music at the same time.

17. Don't back the lady throughout the dance.

18. Ladies follow; don't lead; this is the man's responsibility.

LEADING AND FOLLOWING

1. Keep your body parallel to your partner's.

2. Learn to relax. Hold partner lightly, not tensely.

3. Men start with the left foot, girls with the right foot.

4. Keep your body in a position in which you are looking over your partner's right shoulder.

5. Lead strongly with your right hand and slightly with your left hand.

6. Always cue the lady in advance of the actual move. It's like giving signals when driving a car. If the signal is given too far in advance or not far enough, the one being signaled may not interpret the cue accurately.

7. Ladies, move on the balls of your feet, be alert, and shift your weight as needed to follow the lead. Don't be as difficult to lead as a truck is to drive; have power steering.

THE FOX TROT AND ITS VARIATIONS

The fox trot had its beginnings in the redowa, galop, gallopade, racket, two-step, and the "animal" and "fowl" dances such as the bunny hug, turkey trot, lame duck, and grizzly bear. The analyses of some of the forerunners of the fox trot may be helpful.

FORERUNNERS OF THE FOX TROT

Galop. The galop is a very simple movement composed of slides and changes and danced in 2/4 time. In some quarters, it has been named the "ignoramus waltz." Facing straight ahead, take a series of slide steps sideward, forward, backward, or in any combination of movements. The beginner might practice four slides to the left then four to the right. After mastering this movement, practice two slides in each direction; *slide, change weight, slide* to each measure of music. After mastering these movements, execute them while the body is turned half-way around, a face-to-face, back-to-back movement. The galop is an essential part of many other dance steps. Anyone who can do it while moving in various directions will find most other social dance movements easier to learn. The two-step is a galop with a change of direction for each measure. The origin of the galop has been claimed by both Hungary and Germany and dates back to the early 1800's.

Gallopade. The gallopade is the same as the galop with the exception that there are more than four slides done in one direction before the direction is changed.

Galop racket. This movement requires one slide and two quick changes to each measure of music.

Two-step. Around 1900 the most popular social dance step was the two-step. It is a galop with a change of direction at the beginning of each measure. The two-step can be danced in either 2/4 or 4/4 time. It is perhaps the easiest of all social dance steps to learn. It is a *step, close, step* in one direction, followed by the same movement in the opposite direction.

The term "two-step" is a misnomer, because it has three changes of weight. This term was applicable when the step was performed to music in 2/4 time. When it was adapted to 4/4 time, however, the term was no longer accurate.

The hold that the two-step and waltz had on social dancing was broken by a number of dance fads around the turn of the century.

One-step. Also popular around 1900 was the one-step. It consisted of a step being taken to each beat of a lively 2/4 rhythm.

Fox trot. Harry Fox, a musical comedy star, is credited with the creation of the fox trot around 1913. Dance teachers changed the step and eliminated most of the quick running steps of Fox's original dance. The two-step or chassé movement was incorporated into the fox trot, and this added needed variety to the dance. (Hostetler, p. 89.) The fox trot can be fast, medium, or slow. The music is in 4/4 time and may vary from 28 to 60 measures per minute. Without a doubt, it is the most popular social dance step in the United States.

FOX TROT STEPS

The basic movement pattern for the fox trot is a series of quick and slow dance steps. "Quick" and "slow" refer to the length of time the foot remains off the floor.

The steps most often used are as follows:

Step I. Start with feet together. (See Figure 1.)

1. Slow left step forward.
2. Slow right step forward.
3. Quick left to left side.
4. Quick right to side of left foot.

The step may be repeated, or, if weight is not taken on Step 4, the step may be started with the right foot.

The step may be executed by making all steps the same—slow.

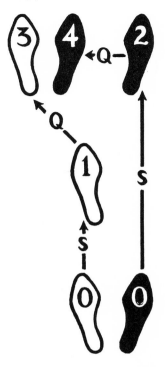

Figure 1: Fox trot step I.

Step II. Start with feet together. (See Figure 2).

1. Quick left to side.
2. Quick right to side of left foot.
3. Slow left forward.
4. Slow right forward.

Repeat as often as desired. This is perhaps the most popular of the fox trot steps.

Step III. Start with feet together. (See Figure 3.)

1. Slow left forward.
2. Slow right forward.
3. Quick left to side.
4. Quick right to side of left.
5. Quick left in place.

Repeat the step leading with the right foot.

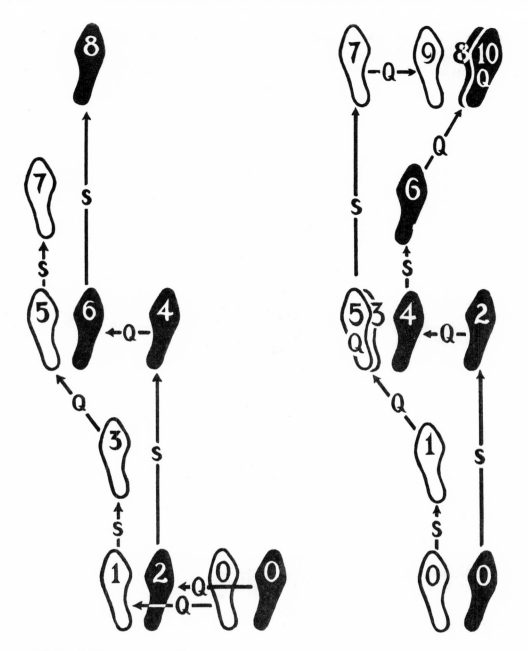

Figure 2: Fox trot step II.   *Figure 3: Fox trot step III.*

Step IV. Start with feet together. (See Figure 4.)

1. Quick left to side.
2. Quick right to side of left.
3. Slow left forward.
4. Quick right to side.
5. Quick close with left to right.
6. Slow right forward.

Continue same pattern.

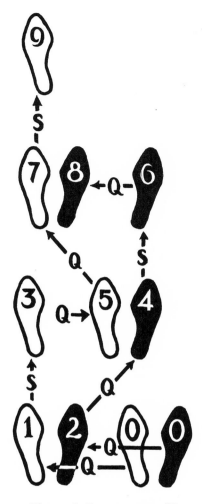

Figure 4: Fox trot step IV.

Step V. Start with feet together. (See Figure 5.)

    1. Slow left forward.
    2. Slow right forward.
    3. Quick left to side of right.
    4. Quick right in place.

Repeat the step going backward, leading with the left foot.

These are some of the most popular fox trot steps. The dancer should mix them up, never repeating any one step over and over. Quarter turns, half turns, walking steps, and swinging of the partner make the fox trot an enjoyable dance step.

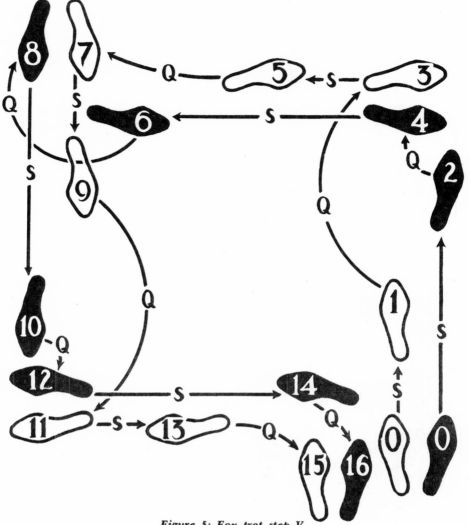

Figure 5: Fox trot step V.

THE CHARLESTON

The Charleston was first done in the 1890's, but reached its maturity and greatest popularity in the 1920's. The Charleston is certainly recreational in nature and has been tried by most dancers at some time. The basic step is simple and easy to learn. The more advanced movements require considerable practice before skill is perfected.

The Charleston is done in highly syncopated 4/4 time, which produces a jerky staccato movement. (White, p. 49.) The basic step is as follows:

1. Step forward left.
2. Point right toe forward.
3. Step back on right.
4. Point left toe back.

The leg bearing body weight is always bent slightly. Practice this movement until you can maintain it with rhythm. Then try to twist both ankles on each step. This is a basic characteristic of the Charleston.

Additional kicks and movements may be incorporated into this dance after the basic fundamentals are mastered.

JITTERBUG

The jitterbug includes a host of variations that made their appearance as people began to tire of the Charleston. Each locality seems to have its own version of these steps, which are believed to have originated with the American Negro. It is done in 4/4 time and is characterized by slow, slow, quick, quick movements. Some of the characteristic jitterbug variations are described.

The Charleston.

Shag.

1. Step left, hop left, raise right foot or kick across in front of left foot.
2. Step right, hop right, raise left foot or kick across in front of right foot.
3. Quick left in place.
4. Quick right in place.
Repeat.

Single lindy. The lindy is one of the most popular dance steps with teenagers. Its origin dates back to 1927, when Lindbergh made his transocean flight to Paris.

1. Feet together.
2. Dig with ball of left foot; transfer weight to left foot.
3. Dig with ball of right foot; transfer weight of left to right foot.
4. Quick left.
5. Quick right.

Figure 6: The single lindy.

The pattern illustrated in Figure 6 may be practiced as follows:

1. Dig left to side, (&) touch right to left (slow).
2. Dig right to side, (&) touch left to right (slow).
3. Rock back on left (quick).
4. Rock forward on right (quick).

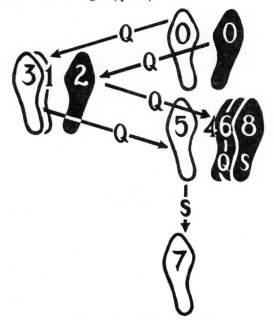

Figure 7: The triple lindy.

Triple lindy. The most popular pattern of the triple lindy may be executed as follows. (See Figure 7.)

1–3. Three fast side steps to left (LRL), two counts. Same as two-step to left.
4–6. Three fast side steps to right (RLR), two counts. Same as two-step to right.
7. Step backward on left (rock or balance back), one count.
8. Rock forward on right, one count.

Most swing, rock 'n roll, and other quick-step innovations use the lindy steps with individual interpretations as a basis for most movements. Keeping in time with the music is the first requisite. The other is doing steps that your partner can follow.

THE WALTZ

The waltz is a graceful dance in 3/4 time. Students of dance give credit to Germany and Austria for their contributions to its development. They gave it form, perfection, and distinction. Johann Strauss and other great musicians made the waltz a symbol of Vienna.

There are several basic movements in the waltz. Those wishing to receive maximum enjoyment from this dance should learn at least four or five different steps and develop the ability to flow from one to the other.

Step I—the basic waltz. Start with feet together, weight on right foot. (See Figure 8.)

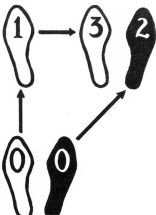

Figure 8: Waltz step I.

1. Step forward on left.
2. Step right out to side, even with left.
3. Draw left foot to right.

Note: Take weight on each step. The next step will be on the right foot, because the weight is now on the left. The step may be forward or backward depending upon the cues of the leader.

Step II—Forward half-square waltz steps. Start with feet together, weight on right foot. (See Figure 9.)

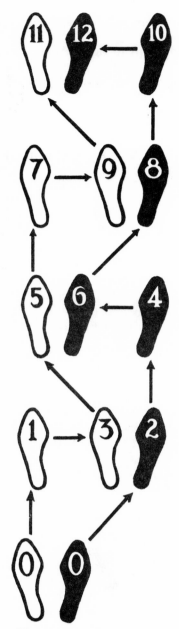

Figure 9: Waltz step II.

1. Step forward on left.
2. Step forward on right, out but even with left.
3. Draw left to right.
4. Step forward on right.
5. Step forward on left, out but even with right.
6. Draw right to left.

Step III—the box waltz. Start with feet together, weight on right foot. (See Figure 10.)

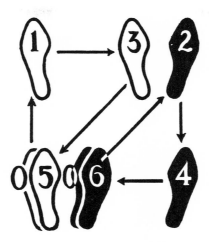

Figure 10: Waltz step III.

1. Step forward on left.
2. Step right out from side of left.
3. Draw left foot to right.
4. Step backward on right foot.
5. Step back on left, out from side of right.
6. Draw right foot to left.

Step IV—Left quarter turns. Start with feet together, weight on right foot. Do a quarter turn on each waltz. (See Figure 11.)

        (1st Quarter)
1. Step forward on left, making quarter turn to left.
2. Step right out from side of left.
3. Close left foot to right.
        (2nd Quarter)
4. Step backward on right.
5. Step left out from side of right as quarter turn is completed.
6. Close right to left.
        (3rd Quarter)
7– 9. Same as 1–3.
        (4th Quarter)
10–12. Same as 4–6.

Step V—Right quarter turns. Start with feet together, weight on left foot. (See Figure 12.)

        (1st Quarter)
1. Step forward on right, making quarter turn to right.
2. Slide left out from side of right.
3. Close right foot to left.
        (2nd Quarter)

Social Dance   205

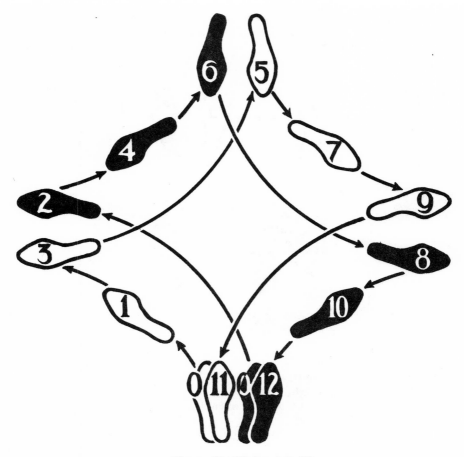

Figure 11: Waltz step IV.

  4. Step backward on left, making quarter turn to right.
  5. Slide right foot out from side of left.
  6. Close left foot to right.
   (3rd Quarter)
 7– 9. Same as 1–3.
   (4th Quarter)
10–12. Same as 4–6.

Step VI—the figure eight waltz. The figure eight waltz step is a combination of left and right quarter turns. (See Figure 13.)

 1–12. Four left quarter turns.
  13. Step back on the left, turning right.
  14. Step to side on right.
  15. Close with the left.
  16. Step forward and turn on right.
  17. Step to side on left.
  18. Close with the right.
  19. Step back and turn on left.
  20. Step to side on the right.
  21. Close left to right.

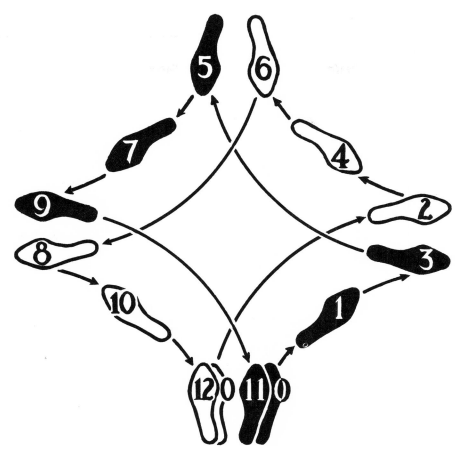

Figure 12: Waltz step V.

22. Step forward on right with turn.
23. Step to side with left.
24. Close right to left.

Step VII—Balance steps. Balance steps are used to shift weight from one foot to the other before a new movement is begun. They are also used as intermediate steps between the left quarter and right quarter turns. And they are used to mark time momentarily while the dancers wait to coordinate rhythmical movements with the downbeat of the music. Start with feet together, weight on right foot.

1. Step forward on left foot (count 1, 2).
2. Touch right foot beside left foot (count 3).
3. Step back on right foot (count 1, 2).
4. Touch left foot beside right foot (count 3).

Step VIII—Scissors step. Start with feet together, weight on right foot. (See Figure 14.)

1. Step left foot diagonally across in front of right (left hip adjacent to partner's left hip. Woman steps backward on right foot).

Social Dance **207**

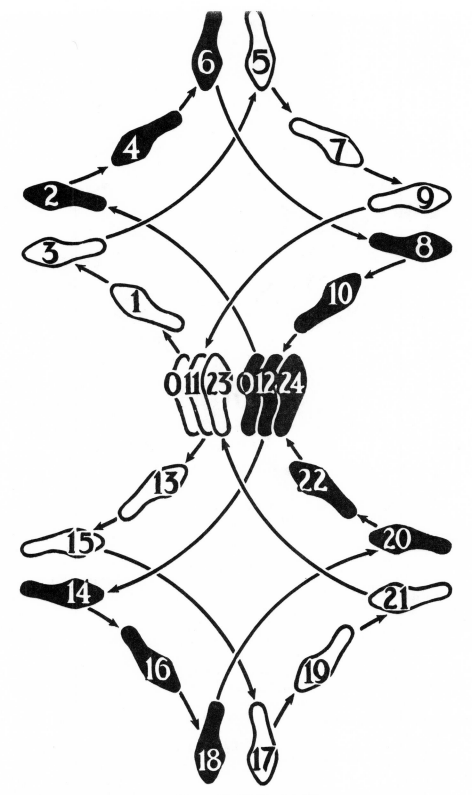

Figure 13: Waltz step VI.

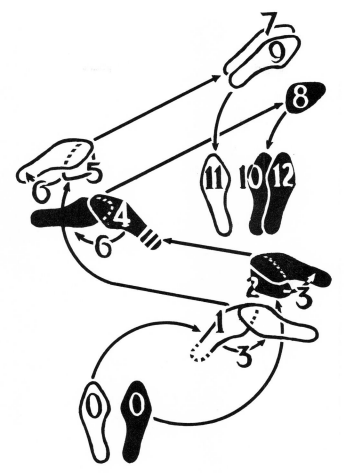

Figure 14: Waltz step VIII.

2. Step right foot just beyond left foot.
3. Turn halfway round on balls of both feet.
4. Step right foot diagonally across in front of left foot (right hip adjacent to partner's right hip).
5. Step left foot just beyond right foot.
6. Turn half around on balls of both feet.
7–12. Repeat 1–6.

This step is frequently concluded with one balance step forward and one backward, assuming social dance position.

Step IX—Pursuit step. This is a pattern of movements in which a small step is taken on each beat of the music. Usually the woman is continuously backing up and the man is following her around the dance floor.

Step X—Serpentine step. Instead of remaining in social dance position as in the pursuit step, body position changes from left hips adjacent one measure to right hips adjacent the second measure. Three or four changes may be made before reverting to a different step.

The rhumba.

LATIN-AMERICAN DANCES

Many of our most popular social dance steps were originated in Cuba, Central, and South America. In these lands there dwells a mixture of races, colors, and creeds. Negroid and Spanish rhythms have influenced many trends in dance. The blending of these rhythms has stimulated interest in syncopation, offbeats, and percussion instruments. The most popular social dances from these countries are the rhumba, the tango, the samba, the merengue, the cha cha cha, the conga, the mambo, and the calypso.

RHUMBA

The rhumba, imported from Cuba, was originally a dance depicting the chores of life. Movements expressed such activities as shoeing a horse, climbing a rope, and courting a girl. The action was somewhat modified before it became acceptable as a recreational dance in the United States. The music and dance steps eventually resembled, to some degree, those of a medium-speed fox trot. Native instruments such as maracas (gourds filled with rattles), claves (two round sticks), timbales (double-headed drums), and bongo drums are used extensively to maintain the syncopated rhythm.

In the rhumba, the center of movement should always be in the torso and pelvis, never in the feet. The knees and hips are flexible, but the action should not be exaggerated. Each step of the foot uses two movements. One foot makes a step at the same time that weight is being transferred to the other foot. The delayed transfer of weight results in the tilting pelvic movements characteristic of the rhumba. In the first movement of the foot, the knee is bent; as weight is transferred, the knee is straightened. The swaying movements of the hips should be smooth, never staccato. Hip movements are always in the opposite direction of foot movements. When the step is to the left side, the hips move to the right, and vice versa.

Foot movements are small and usually close together. Partners seldom make body contact other than hand positions.

The basic rhythm count is *slow, quick, quick* or *quick, quick, slow*. There are usually two quick steps and one slow step to each measure of music.

The music is in 4/4 time, with the accents on the first and third beat of each measure. Because of the percussion instruments, however, the rhythm may appear to be eight beats to the measure. The basic walking rhumba follows. (See Figure 15.)

1. Left forward (slow), hips move right.
2. Right forward (quick), hips move left.
3. Left forward (quick), hips move right.

If the quick steps are chosen as beginning steps, the basic box step may appear as follows:

1. Left side (quick), hips move right.
2. Right close to left (quick), hips move left.
3. Left forward (slow), hips move right.
4. Right side (quick), hips move left.
5. Left close to right (quick), hips move right.
6. Right backward (slow), hips move left.

TANGO

The tango from Argentina was the first of the South American social dances to become accepted in the United States. It has distinct qualities and can be enjoyed by people who know how to do only the basic steps. The music is written and played in both 2/4 and 4/4 time, with each measure distinctly accented. Usually a basic tango step in 2/4 time extends over two measures of music. The step is shown in Figure 16. Start with feet together.

Figure 15: The walking rhumba.

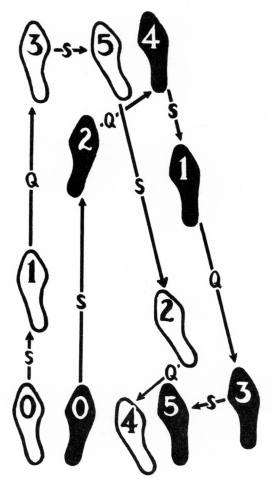

Figure 16: The basic tango.

1. Step forward on left (slow).
2. Step forward on right (slow).
3. Step forward on left (quick).
4. Step right to right side (quick).
5. Close left to right (slow).

1. Step backward on right (slow).
2. Step backward on left (slow).
3. Step backward on right (quick).
4. Step left to left side (quick).
5. Close right to left (slow).

Preparation and corte. Tango music lends itself to balances, hesitations, and related movements. One of the most popular tango movements is the corte, often preceded by a preparatory movement. Preparation and corte are shown in Figure 17.

The samba.

Preparation:
1. Step forward on left (slow).
2. Point right foot forward (slow).

Corte:
3. Step back on right (quick).
4. Step back on left (quick).
5. Point right foot forward (slow).

SAMBA

Brazil is the birthplace of the samba. It is usually written in 4/4 cut time, but it is danced as 2/4 time with emphasis on the last beat. It is a lively lilting dance involving the whole body. There are three changes of body weight to each measure of music. All steps are quick steps. The body sways opposite the foot movement.

The basic samba step is shown in Figure 18.

1. Step forward on left (weight on full foot), body sways backward.
2. Step right foot beside left (weight on ball of foot).
3. Step left foot in place (weight on full foot).

Reverse, stepping backward on right foot.

Figure 17: The preparation and corte tango.

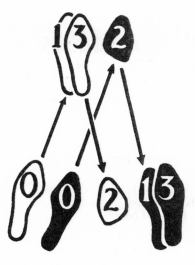

Figure 18: The basic samba.

Figure 19: The walking samba.

The walking samba step is shown in Figure 19.

1. Step forward on left (count 1).
2. Rock weight back on right (count 2).
3. Rock weight forward on left (count 3).
4. Step forward on right (count 1).
5. Rock weight back on left (count 2).
6. Rock weight forward on right (count 3).
Continue forward.

CHA CHA CHA

The mambo and cha cha cha steps seem to be derived from the original Cuban rhumba. Although the mambo has lost its appeal as a recreational dance, the cha cha cha has gained wide popularity throughout the United States. The cha cha cha is written in 4/4 time, and the basic steps are *slow, slow, quick, quick, quick.*
The basic cha cha cha step is shown in Figure 20.

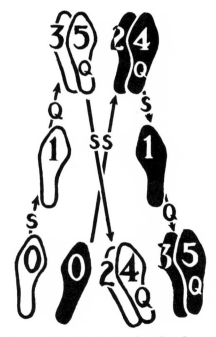

Figure 20: The basic cha cha cha.

1. Step forward on left (slow).
2. Step forward on right (slow).
3. Step left beside right (quick).
4. Step right in place (quick).
5. Step left in place (quick).
Reverse, stepping back on right foot.

The front break is shown in Figure 21.

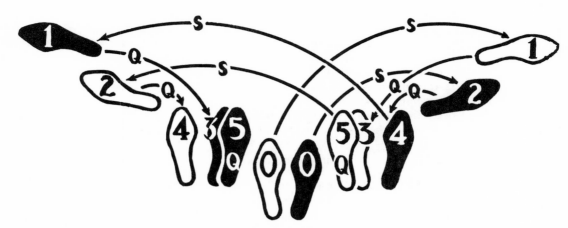

Figure 21: The front break cha cha cha.

1. Step left across in front of right, turning body in direction of step (slow).
2. Rock weight back on right (slow).
3. Step left back slightly, turning body back facing front (quick).
4. Step right back slightly (quick).
5. Step left in place (quick).
Reverse, stepping right foot across left foot.

The cha cha cha chase step is shown in Figure 22.

1. Step forward on left (slow).
2. Shift weight to right while making half turn to right (slow).
3–5. Do three quick steps in place (LRL).

The second step:

1. Step forward on right (slow).
2. Shift weight to left while making half turn to left (slow).
3–5. Do three quick steps in place (RLR).

CONGA

The conga is a Cuban dance of African origin. Its rhythm is played in either 2/4 or 4/4 time and can easily be recognized by the accented beat on every fourth count. All steps are quick steps.

The conga is a circle or line dance done as follows: take three steps in the line of direction (LRL); kick the right foot to the right; repeat the step starting on the right foot.

MAMBO

Some authorities say that the first step of the mambo should come on the second count of each measure. Most dancers make their first movement with the first count. Basically, the steps are *quick, quick, slow.* They may be made in any direction.

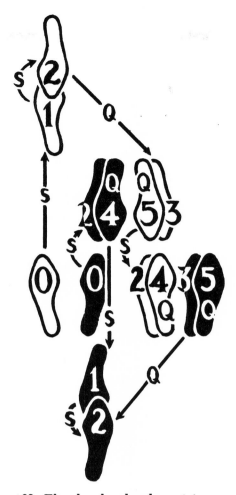

Figure 22: The cha cha cha chase step.

The merengue comes from the Dominican Republic. It resembles the rhumba in its hip movements. The music may be played in either 2/4 or 4/4 time. The basic steps are slow and the movement may be made in any direction. Frequently the steps are in a series and are sidewards.

The calypso originated with the Negroes in the British West Indies. The basic calypso is in 4/4 time. The step movements are *slow, quick, quick.* In the first two steps the hips swing in the direction opposite to the foot movement.

THE POLKA

The polka was first done by Bohemian peasants in the early nineteenth century, and was later introduced into ballrooms throughout Europe.

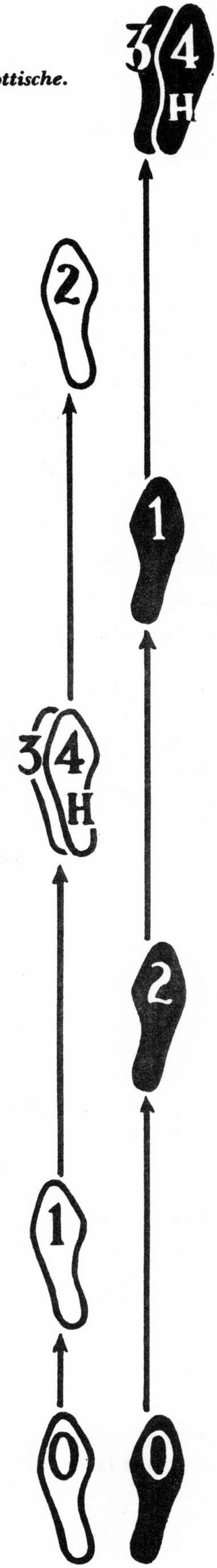

Figure 24: The basic schottische.

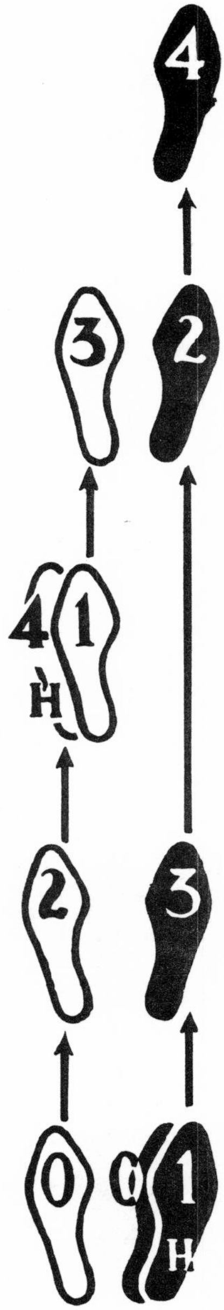

Figure 23: The basic polka.

The basic polka is in 2/4 time, with a lively, uneven rhythm. The foot movement is a two-step with a hop preceding each step, close, step. See Figure 23.

Basic polka moving forward:
1. Hop on right.
2. Step forward on left.
3. Close right to left.
4. Step forward on left.

The second step:
1. Hop on left.
2. Step forward on right.
3. Close left to right.
4. Step forward on right.

This step is often taken sideways. Couples may be in a shoulder-waist position, turning clockwise as they advance counterclockwise around the room.

THE SCHOTTISCHE

The schottische is danced in 4/4 time in a smooth, even rhythm. The step is shown in Figure 24.

1. Step forward on left.
2. Step forward on right.
3. Step forward on left.
4. Hop on left.

Repeat, beginning on right foot. Step-hops may be added during the routine.

Appendixes

formation of a
Dance Club

About eleven years ago, I was asked to present some dance routines for a formal banquet. The routines were simple folk dances. Members of the audience were delighted with the performance and told other organizations about the youthful dancers. Over a long period of time, the club grew in membership, ability, and poise. They learned many kinds of dance, and made elaborate costumes. Invitations for performances grew in number and importance, and eventually the club began to appear on television. Each experience added prestige and luster to the organization, and soon the club organized extensive tours during vacation periods. Each tour opened the gates to additional experiences.

The organization grew to such an extent that many parents, teachers, and specialists were brought in to assist with the countless details essential to the club's rise to national popularity.

This is a brief history of the nationally famous Westchester Lariats. An entire book could be written about their experiences. The following suggestions have been developed from my observations of the Lariats, and should be of help to leaders of dance clubs.

Types of dance. The more types of dance included in a dance club, the greater the interest. It is essential that interest be maintained because skill in dance requires months to develop.

Membership. Membership should be open to people who have physical capability, an interest in dance, and good character.

Practice. Dance clubs should have at least one two-hour practice session each week. Skill and finesse require hours of practice along with regular physical conditioning exercises.

Costumes. Interest increases noticeably when costumes are obtained. The costumes should be kinds that the dancers are not embarrassed to wear. They should be authentic, handsome, and durable.

Performances. There should be enough performances to maintain interest, but not so many that the dancers tire of them.

Pictures and publicity. Pictures should be taken at every opportunity. A committee should be responsible for publicity in newspapers and magazines and on radio and television.

Equipment and props. Each dance club should obtain the very best equipment possible, including records, record players, music scores, tape recorders, and such props as cymbals, castanets, flowers, and canes.

Committees. The larger and more active the club becomes, the more committees it will need. Committees that are usually essential are board of directors, finance, publicity, promotion, costume, hospitality, refreshments, transportation, historical, and orientation.

An active enthusiastic dance club cannot be developed in a few sessions. Interest must grow gradually under fair, firm leadership. Standards must be kept high and deportment outstanding. When problems arise they should be attended to promptly so that members will remain loyal to the organization. With the lively participation of all, the possibilities for accomplishment in the dance club are unlimited.

Glossary of Dance Terms

ACTIVE COUPLE: The couple that is visiting and dancing with the other couple.

ALL AROUND YOUR CORNER LADY: Man goes behind and around the lady on his left.

ALLEMANDE LEFT: Man joins left hands with the lady on his left and walks completely around her.

ALLEMANDE RIGHT: Man joins right hands with the lady on his right and walks around her.

BACK-TRACK: Reverse line of direction.

BALANCE: Bow and curtsy to partner.

BANJO POSITION: Social dance position, right hip adjacent to partner's right hip.

BANJO SWING: Closed position with right sides touching.

BASIC WALTZ TURN: Left quarter turns.

BOX THE GNAT: Man and lady join right hands and exchange places.

BROKEN CIRCLE: Regular circle, all holding hands with the exception of one couple.

BUZZ STEP: A clockwise swing in banjo position with partner. Weight remains on right foot; left foot is used to propel the person around.

CANTER RHYTHM: An uneven 3/4-time rhythm.

CATCH-ALL-EIGHT: All join hands.

CHUG STEP: A push step.

CLOG: Rhythm accented by the dancers' feet.

CLOSED POSITION: Partners facing with man's right arm around lady's waist. Lady's left hand is on man's right shoulder. Man holds lady's right hand in his left hand about shoulder height.

CONVERSATION POSITION: Same as open position.

CORNER: The lady on the man's left.

CORTE: A balance in social dance position.

COUNTERSTEP: Opposite footwork from that described.

CROSS-SKIP STEP: Free foot is brought across in front of the foot supporting the body weight followed by a change of weight and then a skipping movement.

CUT STEP: A quick change of weight from one foot to the other.

DO-PAS-O: Turn partner by the left hand, corner person by the right hand, then partner by the left hand.

DO-SI-DO, DO-SA-DO, DOS-A-DOS: There are several ways to execute this movement. Perhaps the most usual is as follows: In a circle of four, the lady is on the man's right. The men face one another throughout the movement. The two ladies first pass left shoulders. Each then faces and joins left hands with her partner. She circles counterclockwise around her partner, coming back around facing the opposite man. She then joins right hands with her opposite and travels clockwise around him ending facing her own partner. Then she joins left hands with her partner. He places his right hand behind her and in her right hand, which is resting on her right hip. He then turns counterclockwise once around with his partner. Sometimes do-sa-do or dos-a-dos is called at the end of a grand right and left. In this circumstance, the man moves clockwise around his partner, passing right shoulders.

DRAW STEP: Step to one side on one foot, and draw the other foot alongside.

ELBOW SWING: Hook elbows with the person indicated and skip around once.

FACE TO FACE, BACK TO BACK: Partners, moving in the line of direction, turn as they execute prescribed steps so that they are facing each other on one step, then are back to back on the next step, and so on.

GRAND RIGHT AND LEFT: Partners face each other. The men are facing counterclockwise, the ladies clockwise around the circle. Join right hands with partner and pass right shoulders; join left hands with next person and pass left shoulders, continuing all around the circle to beginning position unless instructed to execute some other movement.

GOOSE-STEP: Free leg fully extended.

GRAPEVINE: Step to side, step behind with trailing foot, step to side, and step in front with trailing foot.

HEAD COUPLE: Couples one and three.

HONOR YOUR PARTNER: Lady curtsies to her partner as he bows slightly to her.

HOP: A transfer of weight to the same foot. Spring into the air, landing on the same foot that was last on the floor.

HUNGARIAN BREAK STEP: Hop on left foot, touch right toe forward, hop on left foot, touch right toe to side, hop on left foot, close right foot to left foot.

HUNGARIAN SWING: Partners in banjo position, right hand on partner's waist, free hands curved overhead, buzz step foot work.

HUNGARIAN TURN: Same as Hungarian swing.

JUMP: Leave the floor on both feet and land with weight on both feet.

KOLO: Hop on left foot, step on right foot with a quiver or bounce, hop on left foot.

LADIES' CHAIN: Ladies touch right hands as they move from one person to another.

LEAP: Transfer weight from one foot to the other foot, springing through space.

LINE OF DIRECTION (LOD): Line or direction in which the dance moves.

LONGWAYS SET: Couples in a column, men on ladies' left.

MILL: Usually formed by two couples. Join right hands and move CW around the inside of the ring.

OPEN POSITION: Partners side by side facing the same direction. Man's right hand on lady's right hip, lady's left hand on man's right shoulder.

PAS DE BASQUE: Leap to side, touch trailing foot in front, and step on first foot again.

POLKA: Hop on right foot, step on left foot, close right to other foot, and step on left foot (see pages 217–219).

PROMENADE: Partners marching side by side counterclockwise around the square or around the room. Right hands are joined below joined left hands.

PUSH STEP: As body is moved in one direction, step on leading foot and at the same time push off on the trailing foot.

RIGHT AND LEFT THROUGH: One couple passes right shoulders with the couple they are facing as they exchange positions.

ROLL: In a rhythmical movement turn completely around.

ROUND DANCE: Couple, circle, and team dances characterized by a set pattern and movement.

SASHAY: Man moves sideways counterclockwise around partner. Lady moves in opposite direction to the man.

SCHOTTISCHE STEP: Step one, two, three, and hop on the foot that took the third step (see page 219).

SEE-SAW: Lady moves slightly toward the center of the circle as the man goes around behind her and back to original position.

SET: The square-dance beginning position—four couples arranged one on each side of the square.

SHOULDER-WAIST POSITION: Man's hands on his partner's waist, lady's hands on her partner's shoulders.

SHOULDER-WAIST TURN: Turn in shoulder-waist position.

SIDE-CAR POSITION: Hands in social dance position, left hip adjacent to partner's left hip.

SIDE COUPLES: Couples two and four.

SKATER'S POSITION: Left hands joined in promenade position, man's right hand resting in lady's left hand and placed on her right hip.

SLIDE: A gliding sideward movement on the advancing foot and a quicker closing step with the other foot.

SLIP: Sideward slide.

SOCIAL DANCE POSITION: See closed position.

STAR BY THE RIGHT: Join right hands and move completely around to original position.

STEP-HOP: Take a step, then hop on the same foot.

SWING (BUZZ SWING): Hands in social dance position, right hip adjacent to partner's right hip, using a buzz step.

TAG: Ending dance movement to an added phrase sometimes found at the end of a piece of music.

TOE-HEEL STEP: Generally executed by hopping on one foot and touching the toe of the free foot foreward, hopping again on the same foot and touching the heel forward.

TURN SINGLE: A clockwise turn in four steps.

TWO-STEP: Step, close, step.

VARSOUVIENNE POSITION: Partners facing the same direction, lady on the man's right. Man's left arm extends across behind lady's shoulders as he holds her right hand; left hands joined shoulder height.

WALTZ: Step left, step right, close left to right foot.

WINDOW: Right hip adjacent to partner's right hip, right hands joined above the shorter person's head, elbows pushed forward to partner's shoulder, left hands joined through the triangular opening created by the right arms.

References

Armstrong, Lucile, *Dances of Portugal* (New York: Chanticleer Press Inc., 1948).

Burchenal, Elizabeth, *Folk Dances of Denmark* (New York: G. Schirmer, 1940).

————, *Folk-dances of Germany* (New York: G. Schirmer, 1938).

California Folk Dance Federation, *Dances from Far and Near,* Volumes 1–8 (Berkeley: California Book Co., Ltd.).

Dolmetsch, Mabel, *Dances of England and Portugal* (London: Routledge & Kegan Paul Ltd., 1949).

Domon, S. Foster, *The History of Square Dancing* (Barre: Barre Gazette, 1957).

Duggan, Anne S., *Tap Dances* (New York: A.S. Barnes and Company, 1933).

————, *Tap Dances for School and Recreation* (New York: A.S. Barnes and Company, 1948).

———— et al., *Folk Dances of the British Isles* (New York: A.S. Barnes and Company, 1948).

————, *Folk Dances of European Countries* (New York: A.S. Barnes and Company, 1948).

————, *Folk Dances of Scandinavia* (New York: A.S. Barnes and Company, 1948).

Durant, Will, *Caesar and Christ* (New York: Simon and Schuster, 1944).

————, *Our Oriental Heritage* (New York: Simon and Schuster, 1935).

————, *The Life of Greece* (New York: Simon and Schuster, 1939).

————, *The Reformation* (New York: Simon and Schuster, 1957).

Encyclopaedia Britannica, Volume 7 (Chicago: Encyclopaedia Britannica, Inc., 1958).

Ferrero, Edward, *The Art of Dancing* (New York: Dick and Fitzgerald, 1859).

Fox, Grace I., and Kathleen G. Merrill, *Folk Dancing in High School and College* (New York: A.S. Barnes and Company, 1944).

Frost, Helen, *Tap, Caper and Clog* (New York: A.S. Barnes and Company, 1933).

Galanti, Beanca M., *Dances of Italy* (New York: Chanticleer Press, 1950).

Grindea, Miron, and Carola Grindea, *Dances of Rumania* (New York: Crown Publishers, 1952).

Handy Play Party Book (Delaware, Ohio: Cooperative Recreation Service, 1940).

Harris, Jane, Anne Pittman, and Marlys S. Waller. *Dance A While* (Minneapolis: Burgess Publishing Company, 1955).

Haskell, Arnold, *The Wonderful World of Dance* (Garden City: Garden City Books, 1960).

H'Doubler, Margaret N., *Dance: A Creative Art Experience* (Madison: University of Wisconsin Press, 1959).

Heikel, Inguar, and Anni Collan, *Dances of Finland* (New York: Chanticleer Press, 1950).

Herman, Michael, *Folk Dances for All* (New York: Barnes & Noble, Inc., 1947).

Hillas, Marjorie, and Marian Knighton, *Athletic Dances and Simple Clogs* (New York: A.S. Barnes and Company, 1926).

Hostetler, Lawrence A., *Walk Your Way to Better Dancing* (New York: A.S. Barnes and Company, 1952).

Hungerford, Mary Jane, *Creative Tap Dancing* (Englewood Cliffs, N. J.: Prentice-Hall, Inc., 1939).

Karpeles, Maud, and Lois Blake, *Dances of England and Wales* (New York: Chanticleer Press, 1951).

Kinney, Troy, and Margaret West, *The Dance* (New York: Frederick A. Stokes Company, 1924).

Kraus, Richard, *Folk Dancing* (New York: The Macmillan Company, 1962).
————, *Square Dances of Today and How To Call Them* (New York: A.S. Barnes and Company, 1950).

La Salle, Dorothy, *Rhythms and Dances for Elementary Schools* (New York: A.S. Barnes and Company, 1951).

Lawson, Joan, *European Folk Dance* (London: Sir Isaac Pitman and Sons, Ltd., 1959).

Murray, Arthur, *How To Become a Good Dancer* (New York: Simon and Schuster, 1959).

Nelson's Encyclopedia, Volume 13 (Chicago: Columbia Educational Books, Inc., 1940).

O'Gara, Shiela, *Tap It* (New York: A.S. Barnes and Company, 1937).

Owens, Lee, and Viola Ruth, *Advanced Square Dances* (Palo Alto, Calif.: Pacific Books, 1950).

Rath, Emil, *The Folk Dance in Education* (Minneapolis: Burgess Publishing Company, 1939).

Rice, Emmett A., *et al., A Brief History of Physical Education* (New York: Ronald Press Company, 1958).

Ryan, Grace L., *Dances of Our Pioneers* (New York: A.S. Barnes and Company, 1939).

Sachs, Curt, *World History of the Dance* (New York: W.W. Norton & Company, Inc., 1957).

Shaw, Lloyd, *Cowboy Dances* (Caldwell, Idaho: The Caxton Printers, Ltd., 1939).

————, *The Round Dance Book*. (Caldwell: The Caxton Printers, Ltd., 1948).

Shawn, Ted, *Dance We Must* (Lee, Massachusetts, 1948).

————, *Gods Who Dance* (New York: E.P. Dutton & Company, 1929).

Terry, Walter, *Dance In America* (New York: Harper & Brothers, 1956).

Tolentino, F. R., *Philippine National Dances* (Silver Burdett Company, 1946).

Tolman, Beth, and Ralph Page, *The Country Dance Book* (Weston, Vermont: The Countryman Press, 1937).

Turner, Margaret J., *Dance Handbook* (Englewood Cliffs, N. J.: Prentice-Hall, Inc., 1959).

Urlin, Ethel L.H., *Dancing Ancient and Modern* (New York: Appleton-Century-Crofts, Inc., 1914).

Van Dalen, Deobold B., *A World History of Physical Education* (Englewood Cliffs, N. J.: Prentice-Hall, Inc., 1953).

Van Hagen, Winifred, Genevie Dexter, and Jesse Feiring Williams, *Physical Education in the Elementary Schools* (Sacramento: California State Department of Education, 1951).

White, Betty, *Teen-Age Dance Book* (New York: David McKay Company, 1952).

Woody, Thomas, *Life and Education in Early Societies* (New York: The Macmillan Company, 1949).

World Book, Volume 4 (Chicago: Field Enterprises Educational Cooperation, 1960).

————, Volume 26 (Chicago: Field Enterprises Educational Cooperation, 1960).

ADDITIONAL REFERENCES

DANCE PERIODICALS

American Squares, 1159 Broad St., Newark 5, N.J.

California Folk Dance Federation, 190 Country Club Dr., San Francisco 27, Calif.

Dance Magazine, 231 W. 58th St., New York, N.Y.

Dance News, 119 W. 57th St., New York, N.Y.

Let's Dance, 150 Powell St., Room 302, San Francisco 2, Calif.

Sets in Order, 462 N. Robertson Blvd., Los Angeles 48, Calif.

The Folk Dancer, P.O. Box 201, Flushing, N.Y.

Viltis, Vyts Beliajus, ed., 1402 7th Ave., San Diego, Calif.

MAJOR RECORD COMPANIES

ASP Record Co., 1779 S. Crescent Heights Blvd., Los Angeles, Calif.

Capitol Record Company, Sunset and Vine, Hollywood, Calif.

Columbia Record Company, 1473 Burnum Ave., Bridgeport, Conn.

Dash Records, 1920 N. 47th Pl., Phoenix, Ariz.

Decca Record Company, 50 W. 57th St., New York 17, N.Y.

Folk Dancer Record Service, P.O. Box 201, Flushing, N.Y.

Folkraft Record Company, 1159 Broad Street, Newark 2, N.J.

Imperial Records, 137 N. Western Ave., Los Angeles 4, Calif.

Kismet Record Company, 227 East 14th St., New York 3, N.Y.

MacGregor Company, 729 Western Ave., Hollywood 5, Calif.

Methodist Publishing House, 810 Broadway, Nashville, Tenn.

MGM Records, Hollywood, Calif.

Old Timer Records, 708 E. Weldon Ave., Phoenix, Ariz.

RCA (Radio Corporation of America), Camden, N.J.

Recorded Sound, Ltd., 6A Whitehorse Street, Piccadilly, W.I., London, England.

Sets in Order, 462 N. Robertson Blvd., Los Angeles, Calif.

Windsor Record Company, Temple City, Calif.

Classified Index

The dances are listed here in alphabetical order, with added information to help the reader locate dances suitable to the purposes and abilities of the dance group.

Name of Dance	Origin	Degree of Difficulty	Formation	Basic Steps	Page
Ace of Diamonds	Denmark	easy	couple circle	polka	80
Adam and Eve	USA	easy	square	walk	146
Alexandrovsky	Russia	moderate	couples	waltz	92
All-American Promenade	USA	easy	couple circle	walk	56
Alunelul	Rumania	easy	circle	side step	60
American Square	USA	advanced	square	clog	152
Badger Gavotte	USA	easy	couples	walk	69
Bingo	USA	easy	couple circle	walk	59
Birdie in a Cage	USA	easy	square	walk or skip	145
Black Hawk Waltz	USA	moderate	couples	waltz	95
Black Nag, The	England	moderate	longways	walk, slide	100
Bleking	Sweden	easy	couples	step-hop	50
Braid, The (Pletyonka)	Russia	easy	couples	walk, two-step	53
Brown-eyed Mary	USA	easy	couple circle	walk	78
Bunny Hop	USA	easy	line	side kick	54
California Schottische	USA	easy	couples	toe-heel, walk	66
Calypso	British West Indies	moderate	couples	slow-quick	217

Name of Dance	Origin	Degree of Difficulty	Formation	Basic Steps	Page
Carrousel	Sweden	easy	circle	slide step	58
Cha Cha Cha	Cuba	easy	couples	slow-quick	215
Chantez Chantez	USA	moderate	square	walk	170
Charleston	USA	moderate	couples	Charleston	200
Clap and Turn	Slovenia	easy	couples	polka	80
Come Let Us Be Joyful	Germany	easy	threes	walk, skip	64
Conga	Africa	easy	lines	walk, kick	216
Cotton-eyed Joe	USA	easy	couples	polka	68
Cross Over	USA	easy	square	walk	143
Crow in the Cage	USA	easy	square	walk	147
Cshebogar	Hungary	easy	circle	slide, skip	70
Dive for the Oyster	USA	moderate	square	walk	145
Double Clap Polka	Czechoslo-vakia	moderate	couple circle	polka	101
Dubke	Syria	easy	circle	dubke	81
Fado Blanquita	Portugal	advanced	two couples	two-step	110
Figure Eight	USA	moderate	square	walk or skip	146
Fox Trot	USA	easy	couples	walk	196
Fyrtur	Norway	easy	two couples	draw, waltz	70
Gallopade	Europe	moderate	couples	galop, slide	196
Galop	Europe	moderate	couples	galop	195
Garçon Volage	France	easy	square	walk, skip	83
Gathering Peascods	England	moderate	circle	slide, walk	98
Gay Gordons	Scotland	easy	couples	walk, two-step	84
Gay Musician	France	easy	circle	walk, skip	51
Girl I Left Behind Me, The	USA	easy	square	walk or skip	144
Green Sleeves	England	easy	couple circle	walk	54
Gustav's Skoal	Sweden	easy	square	walk	79
Haake Toone	Netherlands	easy	couples	polka	71
Hall's Square	USA	advanced	square	clog	148
Hatter, The	Denmark	moderate	square	walk, buzz	99
Highland Fling	Scotland	advanced	solo	hop	122
Highland Schottische	Scotland	easy	couple circle	step-hop	73
Hineh Ma Tov	Israel	advanced	circle	walk, run	110
Hokey Pokey	USA	easy	circle	walk	50
Honeycomb	USA	advanced	square	clog	175
Hopak	Russia	advanced	two couples	polka	125
Hora	Israel	easy	circle	side step	54
Hot Time in the Old Town Tonight	USA	easy	square	walk or skip	160
Hurry, Hurry, Hurry	USA	easy	square	walk or skip	163

Name of Dance	Origin	Degree of Difficulty	Formation	Basic Steps	Page
Indian Rain Dance	USA	easy	circle	toe-heel	60
Jessie Polka Square	USA	moderate	square	polka	164
Jitterbug	USA	moderate	couples	swing	201
Kalvelis	Lithuania	easy	couple circle	polka	74
Kanafaska	Moravia	moderate	square	polka	91
Karapyet	Russia	easy	couples	walk, two-step	59
Kentwood Schottische	USA	easy	couples	schottische	73
Ken Yovdu	Israel	easy	circle	hop, jump	67
Kiigade Kaagadi	Estonia	easy	couples	step-hop	63
Kinderpolka	Germany	easy	couples	walk, draw step	51
Koja Koja	Lithuania	moderate	couples	polka	88
Korobushka	Russia	easy	couples	schottische	84
Kozacko Kolo	Yugoslavia	moderate	circle	leap, polka	96
La Costilla	Mexico	easy	couples	walk, skip	65
Lady 'Round the Lady	USA	easy	square	walk or skip	143
La Raspa	Mexico	easy	couples	jump, swing	67
Lariat Special	USA	advanced	square	clog	149
Lindy	USA	moderate	couples	slow-quick	201
Little Man in a Fix	Denmark	moderate	two couples	waltz	93
Makedonka	Macedonia	easy	circle	walk	56
Mambo	Cuba	easy	couple	quick-slow	216
Mañana	USA	easy	square	walk or skip	166
Marianne	USA	moderate	square	walk or skip	181
Merengue	Dominican Republic	easy	couples	walk-slow	217
Merry Widow Waltz	USA	moderate	couples	waltz	102
Mexican Hat Dance	Mexico	advanced	couples	stamp	123
Mi Pecosita	Mexico	advanced	couples	polka	115
Misirlou	Greece	easy	circle	walk, grape-vine	79
My Little Girl	USA	moderate	square	walk or skip	165
Neapolitan Tarantella	Italy	advanced	couples	step-hop	117
Norwegian Mountain March	Scandinavia	moderate	threes	waltz	106
Oh Susanna	USA	easy	circle	walk	77
One-step	USA	moderate	couples	walk	196
Oxdansen	Sweden	moderate	double line	side-step	106

Name of Dance	Origin	Degree of Difficulty	Formation	Basic Steps	Page
Patty Cake Polka	USA	easy	couple circle	heel-toe	68
Polka	Bohemia	easy	couples	hop, step	217
Poor Little Robin	USA	advanced	square	clog	169
Put Your Little Foot	USA	easy	couples	two-step	72
Raksi Jaak	Estonia	moderate	threes	polka	104
Rheinländer for Three	Germany	moderate	threes	schottische	104
Rhumba	Cuba	moderate	couples	walk, hold	210
Ridin' Old Paint	.USA	easy	square	walk	171
Rumunjsko Kolo	Rumania	moderate	circle	step-hop	96
Russian Peasant Dance	Russia	advanced	couple circle	polka	127
Sally Goodin	USA	easy	square	walk or skip	144
Samba	Brazil	advanced	couples	samba	213
Samba Square	USA	advanced	square	samba	172
Say Howdy	USA	easy	square	walk or skip	161
Schottische	Germany	easy	couples	step-hop	219
Schuhplattler	Bavaria	advanced	couples	step-hop	129
Seljancica Kolo	Yugoslavia	moderate	circle	hop, step	97
Sellenger's Round	England	moderate	circle	run, slide	97
Seven Jumps	Denmark	easy	circle	skip, balance	55
Shag	USA	easy	couple	step-hop	201
Shoemaker's Dance	Denmark	easy	couples	skip or polka	63
Sicilian Tarantella	Italy	advanced	fours	step-hop	118
Silver Bells	USA	moderate	square	walk or skip	162
Slinging Hash	USA	advanced	square	clog or skip	176
Soft Shoe (Tap)	USA	advanced	couples or solo	tap steps	186
Somebody Goofed	USA	advanced	square	walk or skip	180
Spinning Waltz	Finland	easy	couples	waltz	82
Spinnradl	Austria	moderate	couples	waltz	87
Steiregger	Austria	moderate	couple circle	waltz	95
Sweet Jennie Lee	USA	advanced	square	clog or skip	174
Swing at the Wall	USA	easy	square	walk or skip	144
Tango	Argentina	advanced	couples	slow-quick	211
Tap	USA	advanced	solo	tap	186
Tea for Two	USA	easy	couple circle	two-step	82
Ten Pretty Girls	USA	easy	couples	walk, brush	83
Terschelling Reel No. 1	Netherlands	easy	couple circle	draw step	53
Terschelling Reel No. 2	Netherlands	easy	couple circle	step-hop	66
Teton Mountain Stomp	USA	easy	couples	walk	72

Name of Dance	Origin	Degree of Difficulty	Formation	Basic Steps	Page
Texas Star	USA	moderate	square	walk or skip	147
That Old Black Magic	USA	moderate	square	walk or skip	179
There's a Rainbow 'Round Your Shoulder	USA	moderate	square	walk or skip	167
Tinickling	Philippines	advanced	couples	waltz, hop	119
Troika	Russia	easy	threes	running step	62
Two Gents Swing with Elbow Swing	USA	easy	square	walk	146
Two-step	USA	easy	couples	walk	196
Viennese Waltz	Austria	advanced	couples	waltz	112
Virginia Reel	USA	easy	file	walk	76
Waltz	Germany	easy	couples	waltz	203
Weggis	Switzerland	moderate	couples	walk, step-hop	89
Western Square	USA	advanced	square	clog or skip	155
Wheat, The	Czechoslo-vakia	easy	threes	walk, skip	61
Wooden Shoes	Lithuania	moderate	couples	walk, polka	89

Subject Index

DANCE

This is a volume in the Ayer Company collection

Ashihara, Eiryo. **The Japanese Dance.** 1964

Bowers, Faubion. **Theatre in the East.** 1956

Brinson, Peter. **Background to European Ballet.** 1966

Causley, Marguerite. **An Introduction to Benesh Movement Notation.** 1967

Devi, Ragini. **Dances of India.** 1962

Duggan, Ann Schley, Jeanette Schlottmann and Abbie Rutledge. **The Teaching of Folk Dance.** Volume 1. 1948

————. **Folk Dances of Scandinavia.** Volume 2. 1948

————. **Folk Dances of European Countries.** Volume 3. 1948

————. **Folk Dances of the British Isles.** Volume 4. 1948

————. **Folk Dances of the United States and Mexico.** Volume 5. 1948

Duncan, Irma. **Duncan Dancer.** 1966

Dunham, Katherine. **A Touch of Innocence.** 1959

Emery, Lynne Fauley. **Black Dance in the United States from 1619 to 1970.** 1972

Fletcher, Ifan Kyrle, Selma Jeanne Cohen and Roger Lonsdale. **Famed for Dance.** 1960

Gautier, Théophile. **The Romantic Ballet as Seen by Théophile Gautier.** 1932

Genthe, Arnold. **Isadora Duncan.** 1929

Hall, J. Tillman. **Dance! A Complete Guide to Social, Folk, & Square Dancing.** 1963

Jackman, James L., ed. **Fifteenth Century Basse Dances.** 1964

Joukowsky, Anatol M. **The Teaching of Ethnic Dance.** 1965

Kahn, Albert Eugene. **Days with Ulanova.** 1962

Karsavina, Tamara. **Theatre Street.** 1950

Lawson, Joan. **European Folk Dance.** 1953

Martin, John. **The Dance.** 1946

Sheets-Johnstone, Maxine. **The Phenomenology of Dance.** 1966